# JAZZIN' THE BLUES
## for the intermediate pianist

## by Vince Corozine (a.s.c.a.p.)
### Composer/Arranger, New York
### Member of International Blues Hall of Fame 2013

### Foreword by
### Johnny Morris
#### Jazz Pianist, New York

### Edited by
### Charlie Freeman
#### Jazz Pianist, New York

### Drum Parts by
### Jeremy Lum
#### Producer, Singapore

www.melbay.com/30640MEB

© 2018 by Mel Bay Publications, Inc. All Rights Reserved.
**WWW.MELBAY.COM**

# FOREWORD

*In all my years in music I have never met anyone with more love, enthusiasm and thirst for knowledge than Vince Corozine. While Vince and I were both music majors at the Crane School of Music in Potsdam, N.Y., we spent many hours collaborating on chord structure, bass lines, jazz licks and so on.*

*Although I have arranged for Count Basie, Lionel Hampton and Stan Getz, my experience barely scratches the surface as compared to Vince's lifelong arranging credits. He has explored every aspect of the blues, which will help people who need an organized approach.*

*I feel qualified to comment on Vince's most recent endeavor because my forte is piano arrangements for keyboard, guitar or any chordal instrument that provides proper background, even though my experience in learning jazz was more trial and error.*

*I would have liked to have had a book like this one, that explained things in an organized manner. I learned by experimentation, listening to the great artists on record, and attending live performances where I would sit close to the pianist and absorb everything.*

*Johnny Morris, Jazz Pianist*

Johnny Morris has performed regularly with such jazz luminaries as: **Drummers**: *Buddy Rich, Mel Lewis and Joe Jones;* **Saxophonists**: *Stan Getz, Zoot Sims, Al Cohn, Coleman Hawkins, Scott Hamilton, Frank Wes, and Gerry Mulligan;* **Trumpeters**: *Roy Eldridge, Clark Terry, Thad Jones, Joe Newman, Warren Vache' and Doc Cheatham;* **Cornetist**: *Ruby Braff;* **Trombonists**: *Kai Winding, Eddie Bert and Urbie Green;* **Bassists**: *Eddie Gomez, Ron Carter, Milt Hinton, Bill Crow*; **Guitarists**: *Chuck Wayne, Toots Thielemans, Bucky Pizzarelli, and Gene Bertoncini;* **Vibraphonist**: *Mike Mainieri;* **Vocalists**: *Marlene Verplanck, and Maxine Sullivan. He has recorded four albums with the Buddy Rich orchestra.*

*Johnny has appeared at Jimmy Ryan's, Birdland, New York Playboy Club, Michael's Pub, and Eddie Condon's in New York City, as well as most of the major hotels in New York City, such as the Caryle, Waldorf, Hilton, Plaza and Sheraton to name a few.*

*His piano arrangements have appeared in:* Piano Today, Keyboard, Sheet Music Magazine, *six volumes for* The Steinway Great American Songbook, *plus other projects for* The Good Music Company.

*Johnny is still active in performing in New York, Connecticut and in California.*

# CONTENTS

|  | Page | Audio |
|---|---|---|
| Preface | 6 | |
| Acknowledgements | 7 | |
| Introduction | 8 | |
| About the Music | 8 | |
| **I. HISTORY OF THE BLUES** | 8 | |
|     Example 1: Blues Melody | 9 | 1 |
|     Example 2: Major Scales and Blues Scales | 10 | |
|     Example 3: Pentatonic and Blues Scales | 11 | |
| **II. THE SOUND OF THE BLUES** | 11 | |
|     Example 4: *Groovy Camel Blues* | 12 | 2-3 |
|     A. Blue Notes and Grace Notes | 14 | |
|         Example 5: *Tired Elephant Blues* | 15 | 4-5 |
|         Example 6: Grace Notes | 18 | 4 |
|         Example 7: Resolving Blue Notes | 19 | 5 |
|         Example 8: Resolving Grace Notes | 20 | 6 |
|     B. Drone Notes | 20 | |
|         Example 9: Drone Notes with Moving Notes | 21 | 7 |
|     C. Pedal-Points | 22 | |
|         Example 10: Pedal-Point | 23 | 8 |
|     D. Tremolos and Trills | 23 | |
|         Example 11: Tremolos and Trills | 23 | |
|         Example 12: *Trill Time Blues* | 24 | 9 |
|     E. Syncopation | 27 | |
|         Example 13: *Playful Puppy Blues* | 28 | 10 |
|         Example 14: Syncopation: Anticipation | 31 | 11 |
|         Example 15: Syncopation: Delay of the Beat | 31 | 12 |
|         Example 16: *Strutting Horse Blues* | 32 | 13 |
| **III. BLUES MELODIES** | 35 | |
|     Example 17: A Simple Blues | 35 | 14 |
|     Example 18: Blues Melody 2 | 36 | 15 |
|     Riffs | 37 | |
|     Example 19: Blues Riffs | 38 | 16 |
|     Example 20: *Shuffle Blues* | 40 | 17 |
|     Example 21: Call and Response | 44 | 18 |
| **IV. BASIC BLUES CHORDS** | 46 | |
|     Example 22: Basic Chords Used in the Blues | 46 | |
|     Example 23: Four Types of Triads | 47 | |
|     Example 24: Five Types of Seventh Chords | 47 | |

|  | Page | Audio |
|---|---|---|
| **V. CHORD INVERSIONS** | 47 | |
|     Example 25: Chord Inversions | 48 | |
|     Example 26: *Nervous Monkey Blues* | 49 | 19 |
|     Example 27: *Sneaky Cat Blues* | 52 | 20 |
|     Example 28: Slash Chords | 55 | |
| **VI. LEFT-HAND PATTERNS** | 55 | |
|     A. Boogie Woogie | 56 | |
|         Example 29: Boogie Woogie Single-Note Pattern | 56 | |
|         Example 30: *Oogie Boogie Woogie* | 57 | 21 |
|         Example 31: Boogie Woogie Two-Note Pattern | 60 | |
|         Example 32: Another Boogie Woogie | 61 | 22 |
|     B. Walking Bass | 62 | 23 |
|         Example 34: *Running Rabbit Blues* | 63 | 24 |
|     C. Shell Voicings | 66 | |
|         Example 35: Shell (Guide-Tone) Voicings | 66 | |
|         Example 36: *Barrel Boogie Blues* | 67 | 25 |
|     D. Stride Piano | 70 | |
|         Example 37: Stride Piano Playing | 70 | 26 |
| **VII. RHYTHMIC INTERPRETATION** | 70 | |
|     Example 38: Straight Eighths and Swing Eighths | 71 | |
|     Example 39: *Petrified Parrot Blues* | 72 | 27 |
| **VIII. IMPROVISING THE BLUES** | 76 | |
|     Example 40: Improvising: Outlining Chords | 77 | |
|     Example 41: Improvising: Blues Scale | 77 | |
|     Example 42: Improvising: Rhythmic Approach | 78 | |
|     Example 43: *I Can Do It Blues* | 79 | 28 |
| **IX. NEW CHORD PROGRESSIONS** | 81 | |
|     A. Added Chords | 81 | |
|         Example 44: Added Chords | 82 | 29 |
|     B. Added "Filler" Chords | 82 | |
|         Example 45: Added Filler Chords | 83 | 30 |
|         Example 46: Walk-Up Connecting Pattern | 84 | 31 |
|         Example 47: Walk-Down Connecting Pattern | 84 | 32 |
|         Example 48: *Bouncing Baby Blues* | 85 | 33 |
| **X. BLUES IN A MINOR KEY** | 88 | |
|     Example 49: Minor Blues Scale | 88 | |
|     Example 50: *Funky Frog Blues* | 89 | 34 |

|  | Page | Audio |
|---|---|---|
| APPENDIX A<br>Blues and Country Fills | 93 | 35 |
| APPENDIX B<br>Four Blues Choruses | 95 | 36 |
| APPENDIX C<br>Comping | 102 | |
| APPENDIX D<br>Practice Tips | 104 | |
| APPENDIX E<br>Chord Symbols Used in this Book | 105 | |
| APPENDIX F<br>What Makes a Good Jazz Solo? | 106 | |
| APPENDIX G<br>Jazz Pianists Every Student Should Hear | 107 | |
| APPENDIX H<br>Glossary of Jazz Terms Used in this Book | 108 | |
| APPENDIX I<br>Blues Songs to Learn | 110 | |
| APPENDIX J<br>Select Bibliography of Blues Books | 111 | |
| APPENDIX K<br>Select Bibliography of Jazz Improvisation Books | 111 | |
| About the Author | 112 | |

# PREFACE

The blues is a familiar musical form that all jazz players learn early in their careers. It is probably the most commonly used form in jazz, with countless numbers of recordings by jazz musicians.

The form of the 12-bar blues is AAB and this form cannot be copyrighted (owned) by any individual or company. Melodies and lyrics, however, are copyrightable, while song titles are not. For example there are over 40 songs with the title, "I Love You."

Realizing that most piano students should be exposed to the blues, I wrote this book in an attempt to allow the intermediate pianist the opportunity of playing along with a jazz combo on the accompanying audio tracks (Track 1), and improvising (Track 2).

This book presents 15 original blues songs in various styles; all are offered in a variety of styles such as boogie-woogie, shuffle, rock, gospel, country, and jazz. Each of the 15 blues songs are recorded with an instrumental background including a rhythm section. Of the 50 examples cited in the book, 40 are recorded, enabling the pianist to learn by listening.

A unique aspect of the book is the inclusion of two separate piano parts. Piano (1) is for the intermediate pianist, while Piano (2) is a more advanced part for the teacher. Both piano parts include fingerings for ease of playing. The parts may be performed together and or with the recorded background. The more advanced part, Piano (2) contains more fully-voiced chords, stylistic fills, and rhythmic "comping". *Comping* is a skill using rhythmic patterns for playing chords while accompanying a vocalist or soloist. The Piano (2) part may be learned by the intermediate pianist as he or she progresses.

In an attempt to limit the scope of this book, I have composed 15 original blues songs and other examples in the keys of C, F, B♭ and G major, and one blues song in D minor.

Included in the book are appendices such as: Blues Scales, Chord Symbols Used in the Book, What Makes a Good Jazz Solo?, Comping, Practice Tips, List of Jazz Pianists, Blues, Gospel and Country Fills, Four Blues Choruses in F Major, A Glossary of Jazz Terms, Select Bibliographies of Blues Books, and a list of Jazz Improvisation Books.

This book should provide an understanding and appreciation of the blues and its various styles. It will introduce the student to the blues and will broaden the teacher's understanding of the blues as well.

I wish to thank the following people for their assistance in writing this book:

Jazz pianist, composer, and arranger, Johnny Morris who wrote the Foreword for the book and offered helpful suggestions for improving it. Jazz pianist, Charlie Freeman who edited the book and provided fingerings for both piano parts for all 15 songs, composer and producer Jeremy Lum of Singapore, who wrote the drum parts for the 15 songs, professor of English from Michigan, Charlene Tiffany, who helped edit the book and provided suggestions regarding content and formatting.

Analysis, suggestions, and reviews were provided by pianists: Johnny Morris, Michael Cochrane, Dr. William Bloomquist, and Charlie Freeman.

My love and thanks to my wife Norma, who provided the support, patience and encouragement that I needed to complete this book.

*My special thanks to Bill Bay, President, and Sharon Feldman, IT Coordinator at Mel Bay Publications, Inc., for their encouragement and for publishing my second book.*

# REVIEWER QUOTES

*"Vince Corozine is a master composer and arranger for concert and theatrical orchestras and for jazz bands large and small. Therefore, I was greatly honored when he asked my help in the preparation of this book. I'm thrilled to see how it came out. His work here is a product of a lifetime of experience in the classroom and on the bandstand. As a result, "Jazzin' the Blues" is a comprehensive and easy-to-follow introduction to playing blues in a variety of jazz and pop styles and is ideally suited for both the beginning and the intermediate level pianist. Moreover, with this book Vince has added to his extensive opus of compositions a collection of catchy blues tunes that will be as fun to play as they are instructive. Bravo, Vince!"*

Charlie Freeman, *jazz pianist, New York*

*"Vince Corozine has written a great introduction to the blues for the intermediate pianist. He begins with a brief historical introduction. He then covers some of the fundamental elements of blues playing such as blues scales, pentatonic scales and blues melodies. There are many examples in the book which clearly illustrate his points. He also deals with the harmonic elements of the blues including different types of chord voicings such as shells etc. He also covers different styles of the blues, including boogie-woogie, walking bass lines, stride and a hint of bebop. I was particularly drawn to the advice that was given to players concerning soloing and comping, very sound advice indeed. I believe that Vince has successfully added to the modern library of books on Jazz and Blues. It is a must-read for the aspiring blues and jazz pianist."*

Michael Cochrane, *jazz pianist, composer, arranger and instructor. New Jersey*

"This new book by Vince Corozine is a wealth of information, organized in a very systematic way. The two things that make it most valuable are that it is not a graded method book that a student plays through and discards, but it is a resource that can be used over a long period of time, applying the principles taught in the book, at many different levels of a student's development. In addition, the audio files that come with the book are an invaluable resource, so that a student and teacher can learn by listening as well as from the printed page. The music comes alive when the student gets to play along with the jazz combo."

Dr. William Bloomquist, *pianist-educator, Annapolis, Maryland*

# INTRODUCTION

*Jazzin' the Blues for the Intermediate Pianist* is designed to introduce the young pianist to the blues. The book begins with the basics of blues, such as blues scales, blues form, blues chords, ornaments, chord inversions, blues melodies, left-hand patterns and an approach to jazz improvisation.

Herein are fifteen original blues songs in the keys of C, F, B♭ and G major, plus one 12-bar blues in D minor. These songs are written for the intermediate pianist and progress from easy to medium-easy in difficulty. It is recommended that you practice each hand individually before attempting to play both hands together. Begin slowly and gradually increase your speed to match the metronome mark indicated at the beginning of each blues song. At that point you will be ready to play along with the downloadable audio recording.

# ABOUT THE MUSIC

There are 50 examples in the book, 40 of which are recorded. These recorded examples, including 15 original blues songs, can be downloaded online. An audio icon indicating the track number is inserted at the beginning of each example that is recorded. Each of the 15 accompanying tracks begins with preparation clicks. Track 1 features a solo piano with instrumental background. On Track 2, the solo piano part is omitted, and you are allowed the freedom to improvise a solo. Once you are able to play the solo piano part with ease in both hands, you are encouraged to improvise (make up a melody) using the blues scale to play along with Track 2.

Unless otherwise specified, all music examples in this book are to be played in a swing-eighth style. The accompanying recordings will give you the feel for how they should sound. The student can learn how to "comp" (accompany) by studying Piano Part 2 or by learning to play it.

Fingerings are included in each piano part for ease of learning and playing.

# 1. HISTORY OF THE BLUES

The blues, a truly American form with its unique color tones and embellishments, can be described as a sound, a feeling, a style, or a form. "I've got the blues" describes a state of mind that may have nothing to do with music. It can describe sorrow, joy, humor, tears, or any other deep emotion. It has influenced almost every form of jazz, popular, country and rock music.

The first blues was vocal music, consisting of "field-hollers," spirituals and work songs. Most blues singers received their vocal training in church. Blues songs are usually melancholy in nature and the lyrics typically tell a story about problems experienced by the rural African-American population of the South, with a lover, a job, being lonely, losing a friend, the environment, or any other subject that the blues singer decides to sing about. Sometimes the blues talks about how the difficulties of this present life will become better tomorrow. It is a very emotional kind of music.

The blues style features the call-and-response interchange between voice and instruments, or between the band and soloist. It is a style of performing with extreme freedom of expression, sliding up and down to notes, and employing other forms of inventive phrasing.

Blues melodies are usually in AAB form consisting of three 4-bar phrases that equal 12 measures of music. The A section consists of 4 measures; the second A section is also 4 measures long, and the B section is also 4 measures for a total of 12 measures. Blues makes use of the basic major chords in a key, the I (tonic), IV (subdominant), and V (dominant) chords. The beginning of the first A phrase begins on the I chord (tonic), the beginning of the second A phrase begins on the IV chord (subdominant) and the final C section begins on the V chord (dominant). The melody of the blues has a limited range of notes and usually descends near the end of a phrase.

The only note not used in the blues is the minor second, a half-step above the tonic. This note is too dissonant to work with the blues. You will notice that most blues melodies are in the "call and response" pattern and each pattern lasts approximately two measures.

Iambic pentameter refers to a certain metric line of English poetry, and has to do with the number of stressed and unstressed syllables in the lines. Many of Shakespeare's sonnets were written in this meter. Blues phrases also take on the meter of iambic pentameter.

**Example 1: Blues Melody**

Blues music began when African slaves were brought to North America in the late 19th century and their musical influences permeated every aspect of American music. Blues is a mix of the African beat using syncopated rhythmic figures, with European harmonies and Latin-American influences. Slaves were poor and uneducated and could not read or write the English language, so they had to find a way to communicate with each other while working in the fields. Amid the drudgery and toil of work, the slaves managed to sing and chant musical phrases in a call-and-response style that reflected their living conditions. They used work songs, field-hollers, chants, and spirituals (religious songs) to send messages to one another. Some of the typical work done by the slaves was picking cotton, breaking rocks, chopping wood, driving spikes, and lifting or carrying heavy objects.

As you play and listen to the blues, you will notice that the blues tends to change or lower certain notes in the major scale, such as the 3rd, 5th, and 7th by one half-step. These altered notes are referred to as "blue notes." These "blue notes" usually resolve or move to a note a minor 3rd lower, or to a note a half-step above. The flatted third, flatted fifth, and the flatted seventh are the most commonly used sounds heard in the blues.

For instance, here are the major scales in the keys of C, F, B♭ and G major and their corresponding blues scale with "blue notes" added. The blues scale can be derived by lowering the third, fifth (or raising the fourth), and the seventh degrees of the major scale by a half-step. These modifications are referred to as the "flatted third, flatted fifth, and flatted seventh" respectively. You will notice that the second and sixth degrees of the major scale are omitted in the blues scale.

**Example 2: Major Scales and Blues Scales**

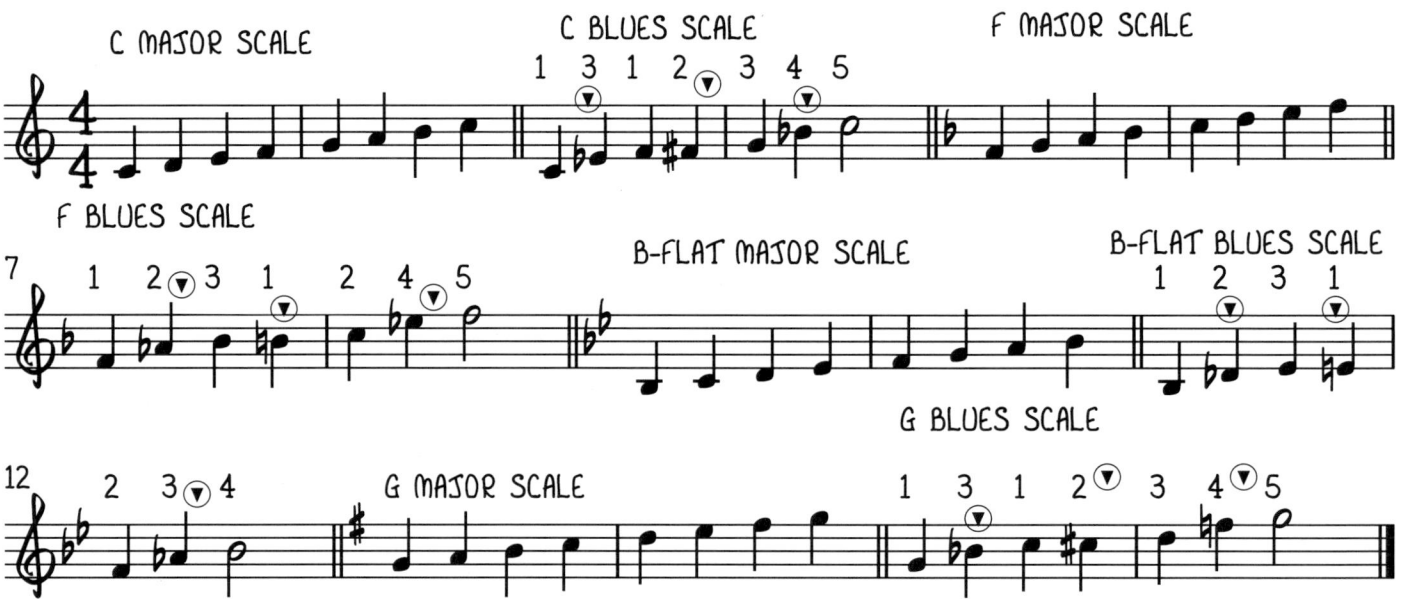

The *pentatonic* (five-note) scale has been used by countless cultures for many centuries. It is the basis of Chinese music. Pentatonic scales are ambiguous in sound and therefore can be used in many different ways in jazz.

During the 1970s, pentatonic patterns and sequences became popular with such jazz artists as Joe Henderson, Chick Corea, and Joe Farrell, among others.

The player has the option of playing a pentatonic scale with the blues. The minor blues scale was used very effectively by many jazz musicians, particularly pianist Wynton Kelly and trombonist Carl Fontana. Here is an example of an F minor pentatonic scale and an F major blues scale.

**Example 3: Pentatonic and Blues Scales**

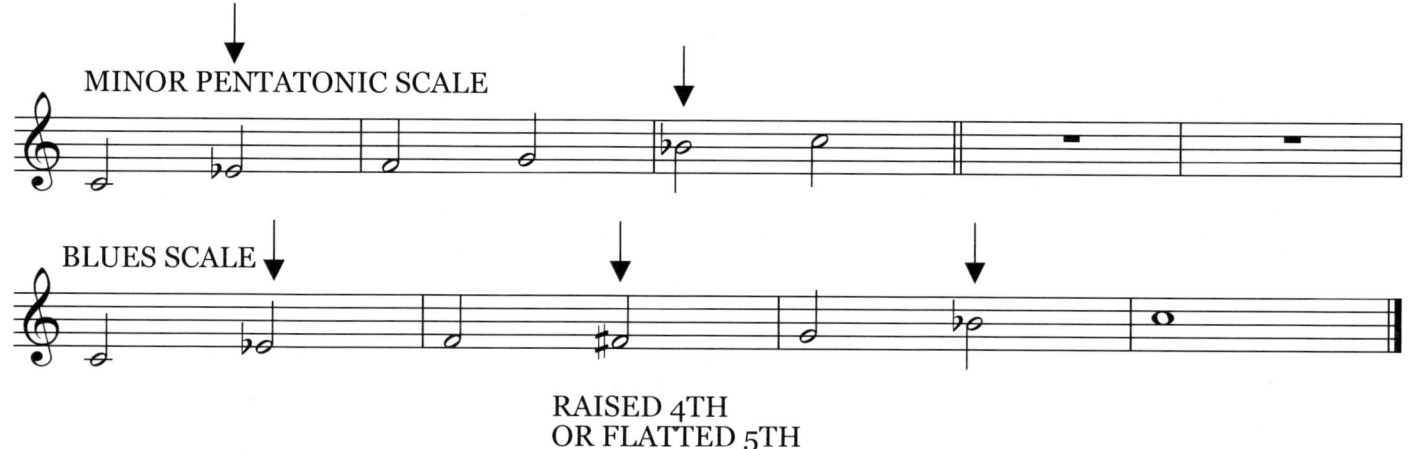

# II. THE SOUND OF THE BLUES

The blues scale is widely used in blues, rock and jazz styles. When one hears the blues sung or played on an instrument, one immediately notices that some notes are "bent" as the performer slides up or down to them, and the melody often creates a dissonance with the background chords.

In the next song, notice that the chords are voiced in root position (i.e. the root is the lowest note in the chord).

**Example 4:** Groovy Camel Blues

# GROOVY CAMEL BLUES

♩ = 116   KEY OF C MAJOR

BY VINCE COROZINE

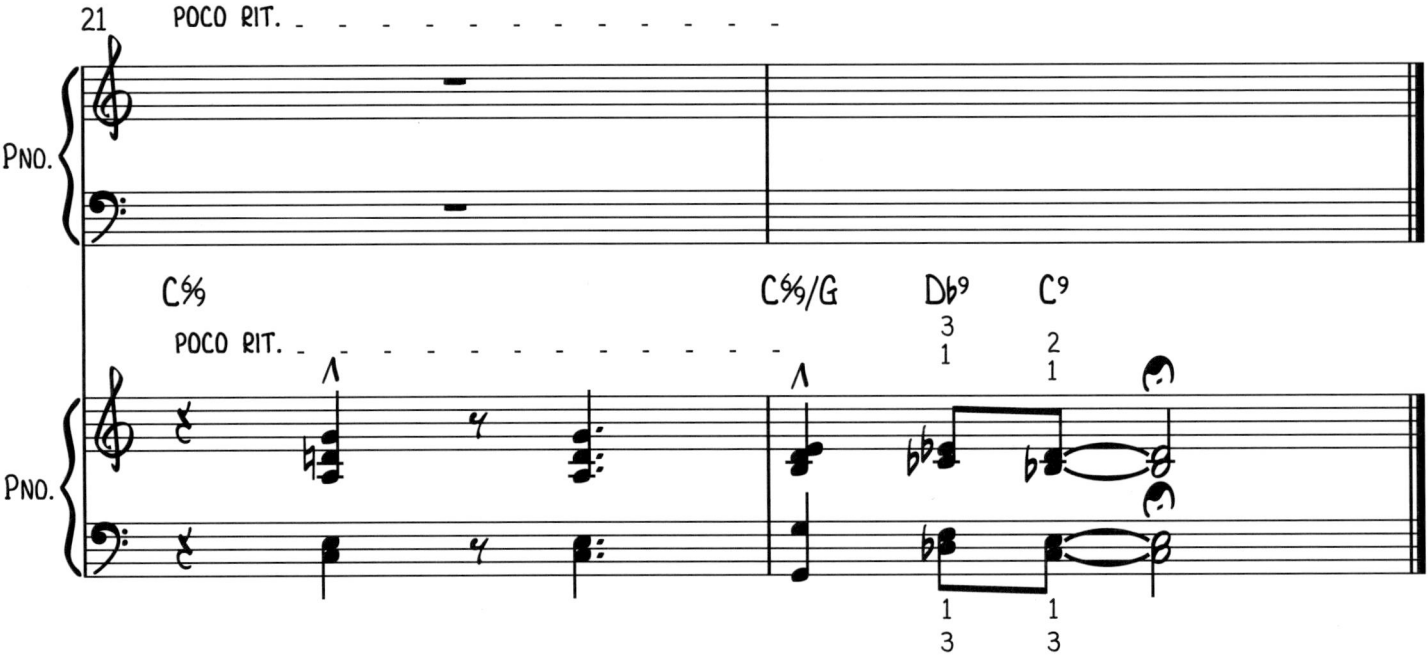

## A. Blue Notes and Grace Notes

The next song, "Tired Elephant Blues," should be played with a 12/8, uneven eighth-note, jazz feel.

The "bent," "crushed" or sliding notes are called *grace notes* and use members of the altered major scale forming a blues scale as shown in the example below. The sliding or "slipping" is characteristic of what a guitarist or banjo player would do. When a pianist wishes to slide or slip up to note, he or she must play a grace note quickly, just prior to the main note to simulate this effect. Grace notes are usually played quickly just before the 3$^{rd}$, 5$^{th}$ or 7$^{th}$ of the chord.

**Example 5: Tired Elephant Blues**

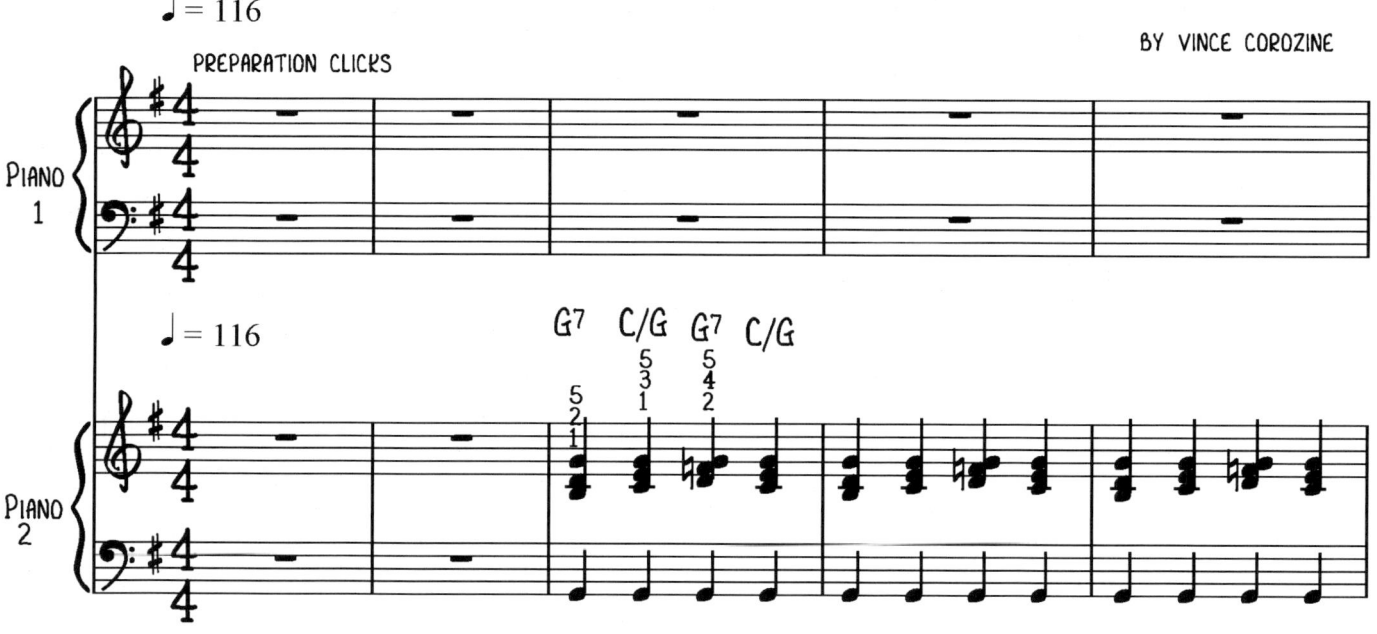

Grace notes are notes that are quickly played just prior to playing a note that is accented.

**Example 6: Grace Notes**

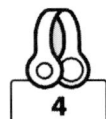

Notes of the blues scale can be played or sung over all the chords used in the typical blues progression. Blue notes sound as though one is striking two notes together, a minor second apart, to form a "twang" or a dissonant *blue note*. Blue notes are also referred to as "crushed tones" or "sliding notes" and have an "elastic" quality. Blue notes usually resolve down a minor third as shown in the next example, while the same notes used as grace notes resolve up or down a minor second to the third, fifth or seventh. To create a real "bluesy" feeling in your playing, relax and lean into beats one and three in each measure.

**Example 7: Resolving Blue Notes**

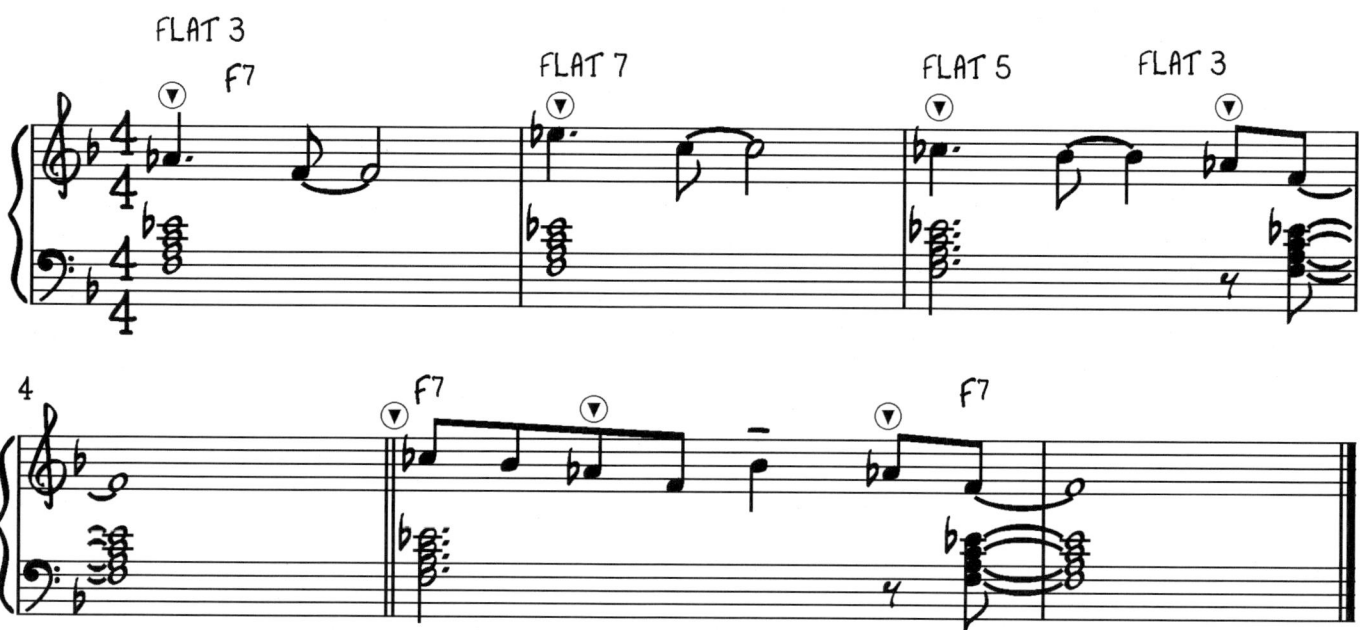

**Example 8: Resolving Grace Notes**

# RESOLVING GRACE NOTES

**B. Drone Notes**

*Drone notes* are repeated or held notes above a moving line or phrase. Notes that move underneath the drone note are usually blue notes (♭3, ♭5, ♭7).

**Example 9:** Drone Notes with Moving Notes

# DRONE NOTES WITH MOVING NOTES

## C. Pedal-Point

A tone held throughout a phrase with no regard for the harmonic motion is called a *pedal-point*, or *organ-point*. This an effective way to fix, or stabilize, a tone (usually the tonic or dominant) in the listener's ear, while the other notes and chords change randomly. The result is accumulated tension and expectation. The pedal-point often clashes with the other parts and surrounding harmonies and most often appears in the bass voice.

The next example has a pedal-point on the dominant note (C) of the F major scale, which intensifies the drive toward the start of the piece.

**Example 10: Pedal-Point**

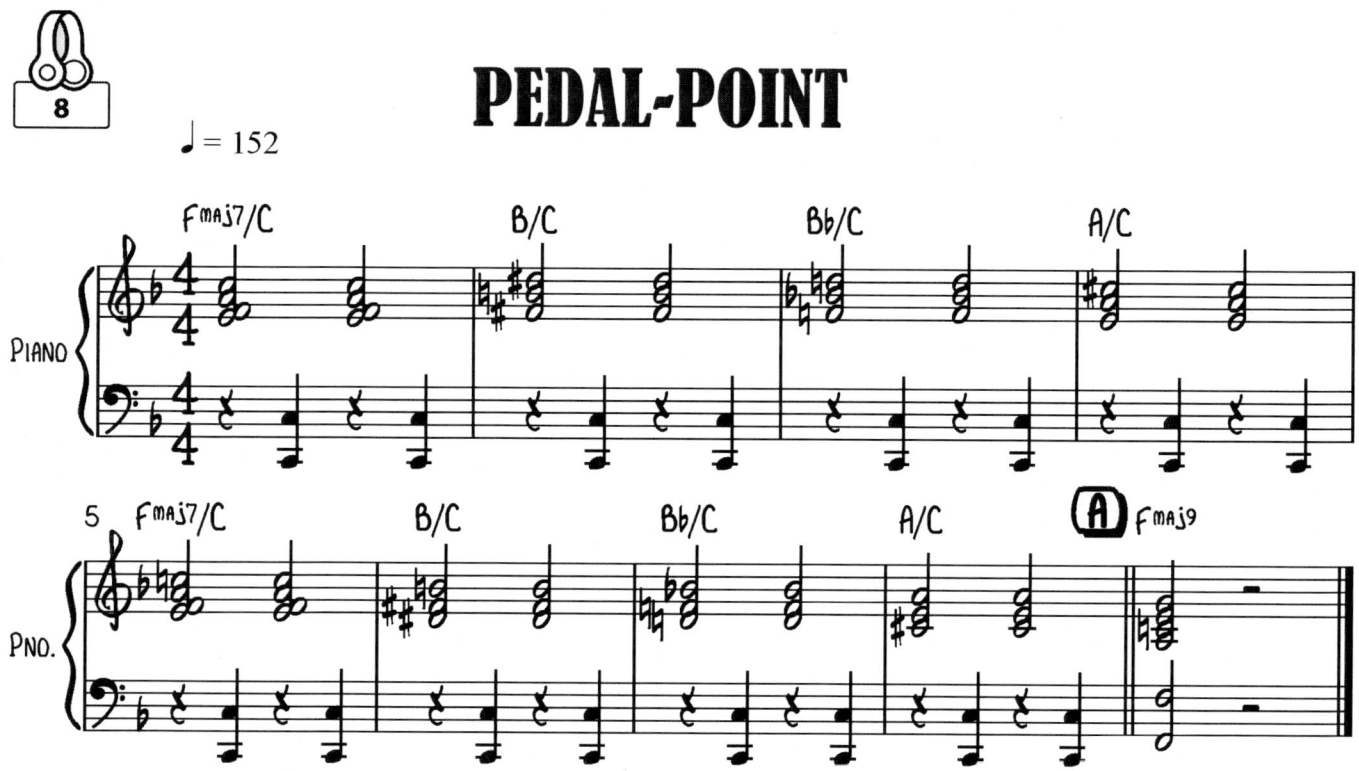

## D. Tremolos and Trills

Most pianists use *trills* (rapid alternation between two notes, usually a half or whole step apart) and *tremolos* or "rolls" (reiteration of two or more notes at a wider interval such as a third, sixth, or octave). Trills and tremolos create excitement and produce a dramatic effect in your playing. They provide color and variety, and are often used in introductions. The sound of trills and tremolos produces a dense effect.

**Example 11: Tremolos and Trills**

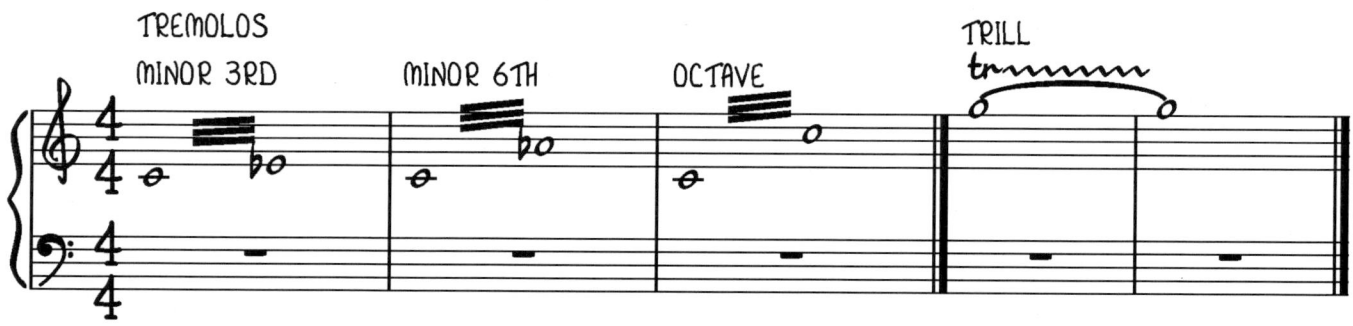

The next song should be played using swing-eighth notes with a 12/8 gospel feel. Observe the sparse open voicings in the left hand. Remember to play the trills evenly.

**Example 12:** Trill Time Blues

# TRILL TIME BLUES

BY VINCE COROZINE

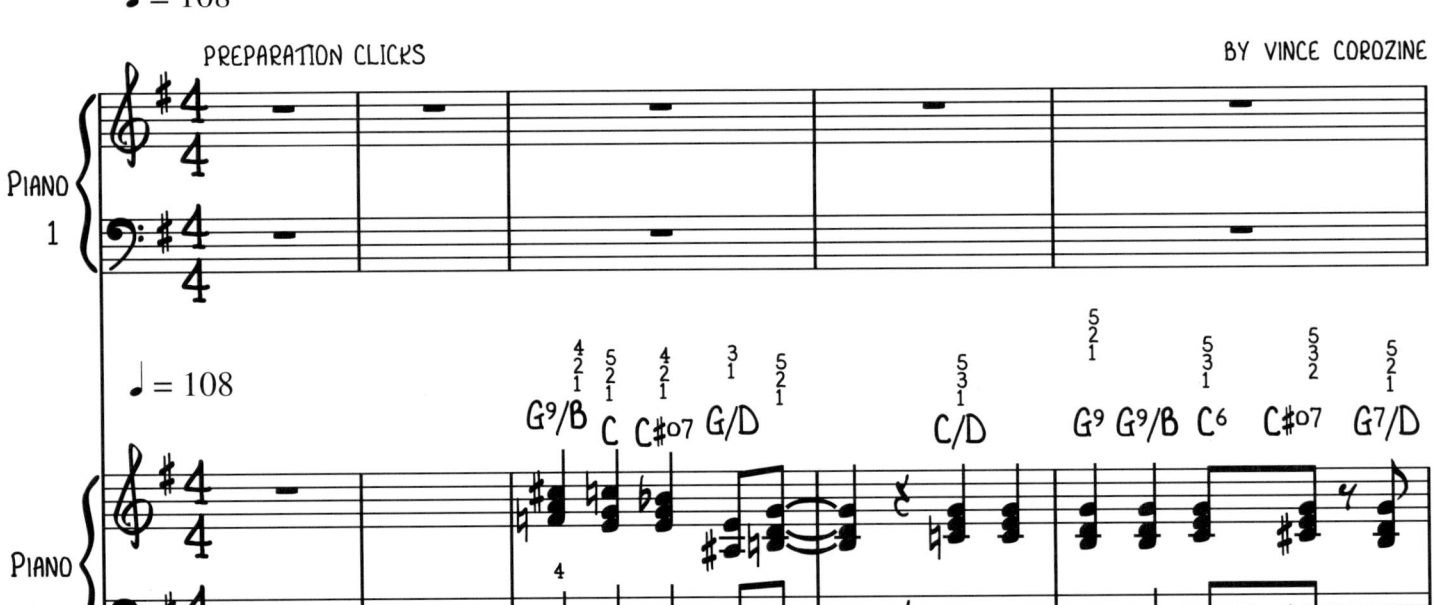

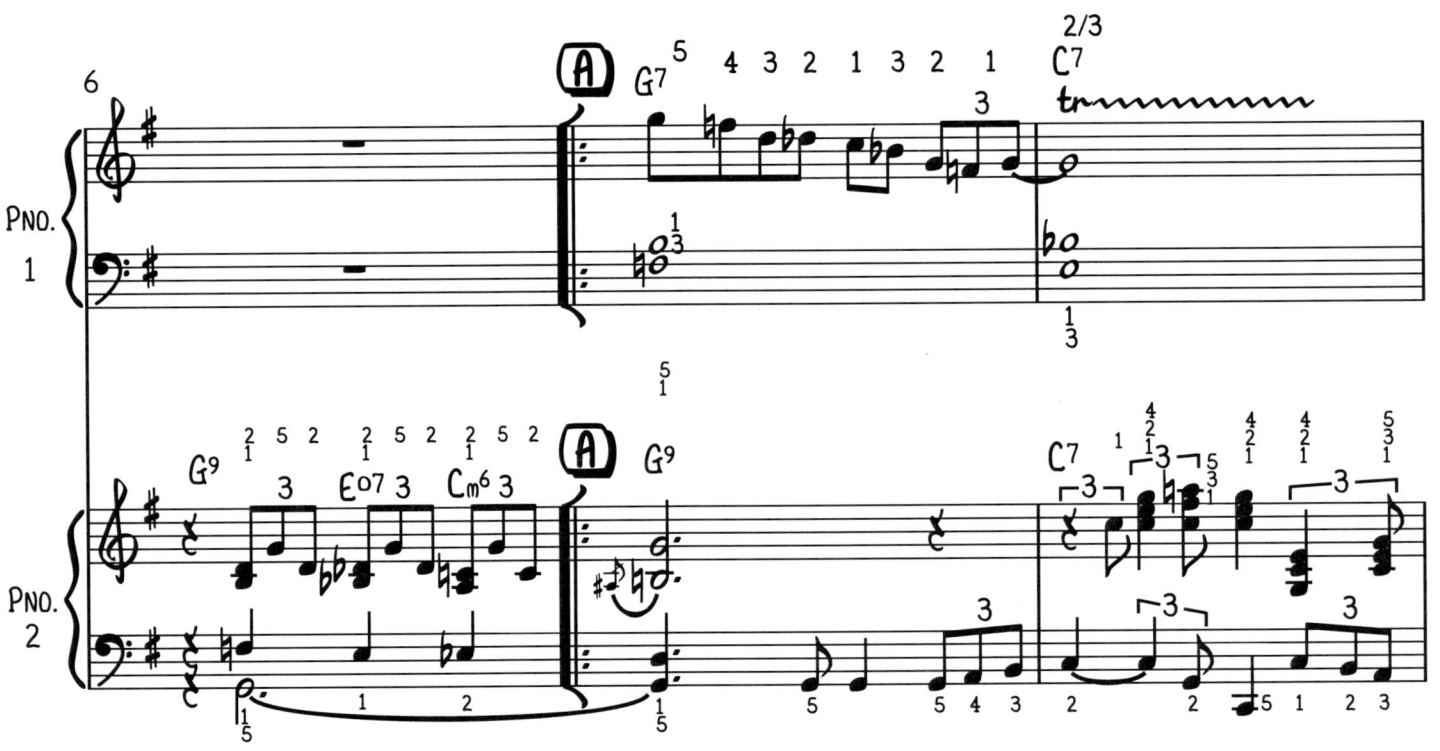

24

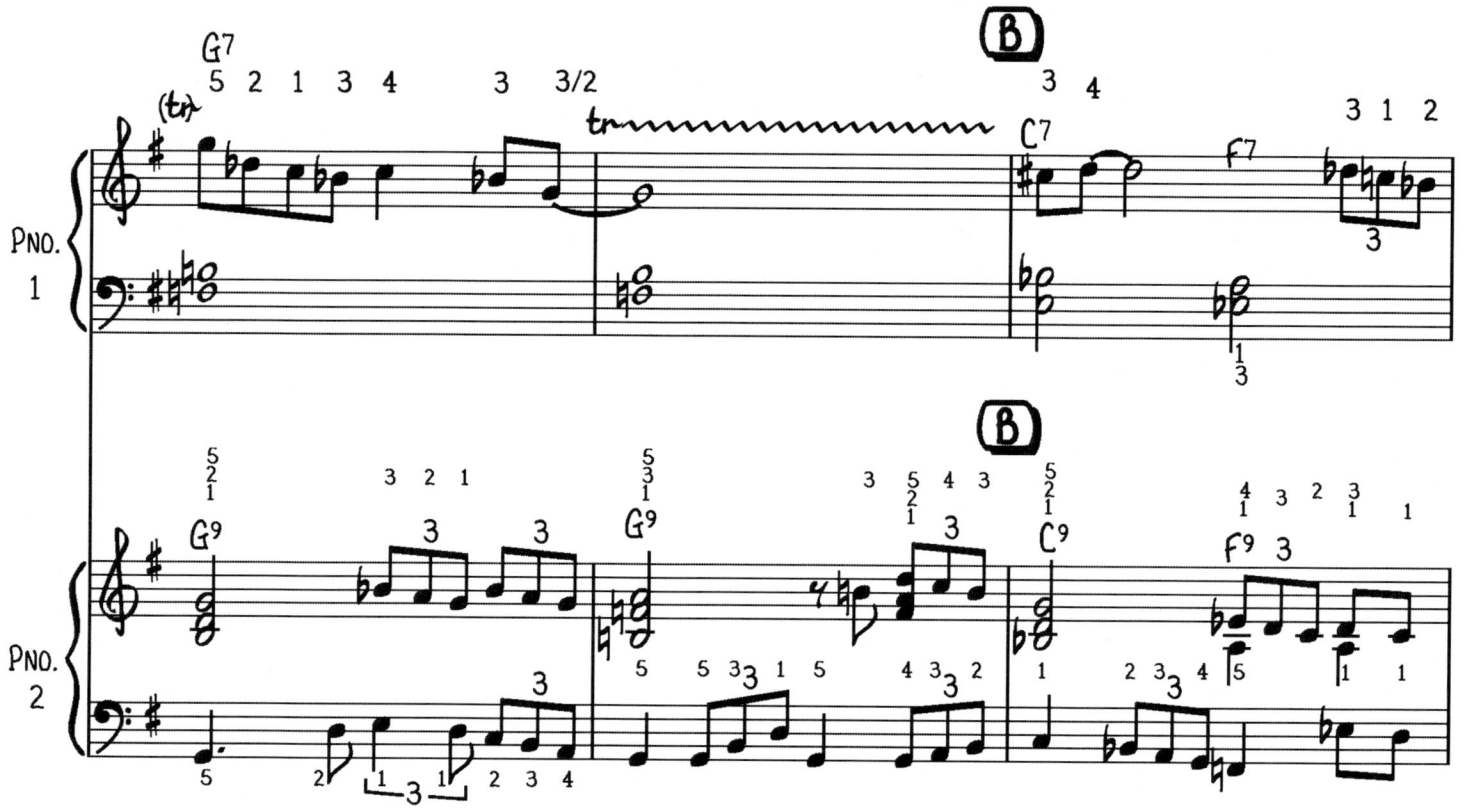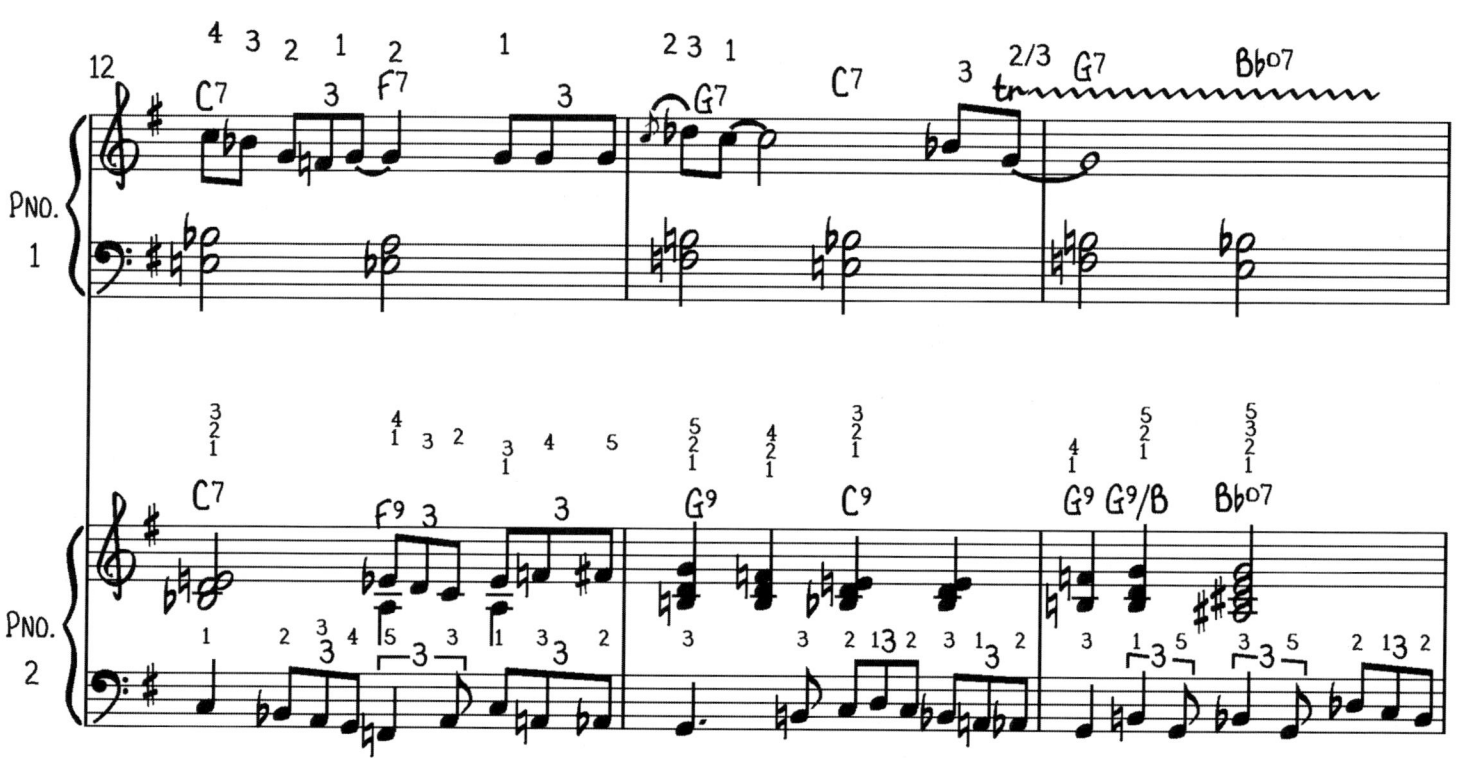

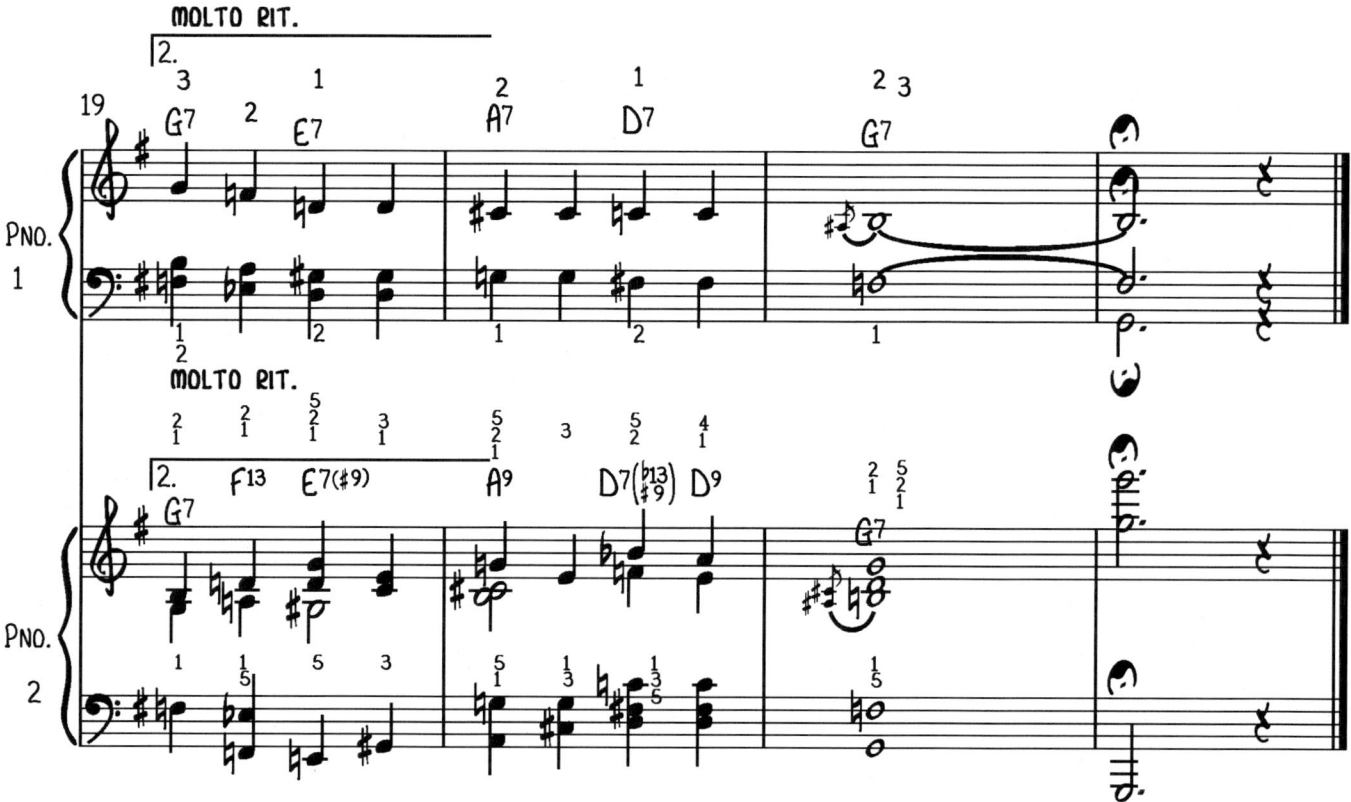

## E. Syncopation

The essence of jazz and blues is rhythmic syncopation. Syncopation refers to the practice of shifting an accent from a normally strong beat to a relatively weak beat. When one plays a march the regular accents occur on beats one and three. If the accents fall on beats two and four, a form of syncopation occurs.

The following examples show what typical syncopation figures look like.

Two of the popular forms of syncopation are:

1. *Anticipation of the next beat*, particularly the anticipation of beat three of a measure. This is achieved by playing a note and holding it through to the next beat.

2. *Delay of the beat*, where the chord or note occurs after the beat.

This song introduces syncopated figures where beat four is anticipated. The left-hand chords are in root position.

**Example 13: Playful Puppy Blues**

# PLAYFUL PUPPY BLUES

♩ = 120
KEY OF C MAJOR

BY VINCE COROZINE

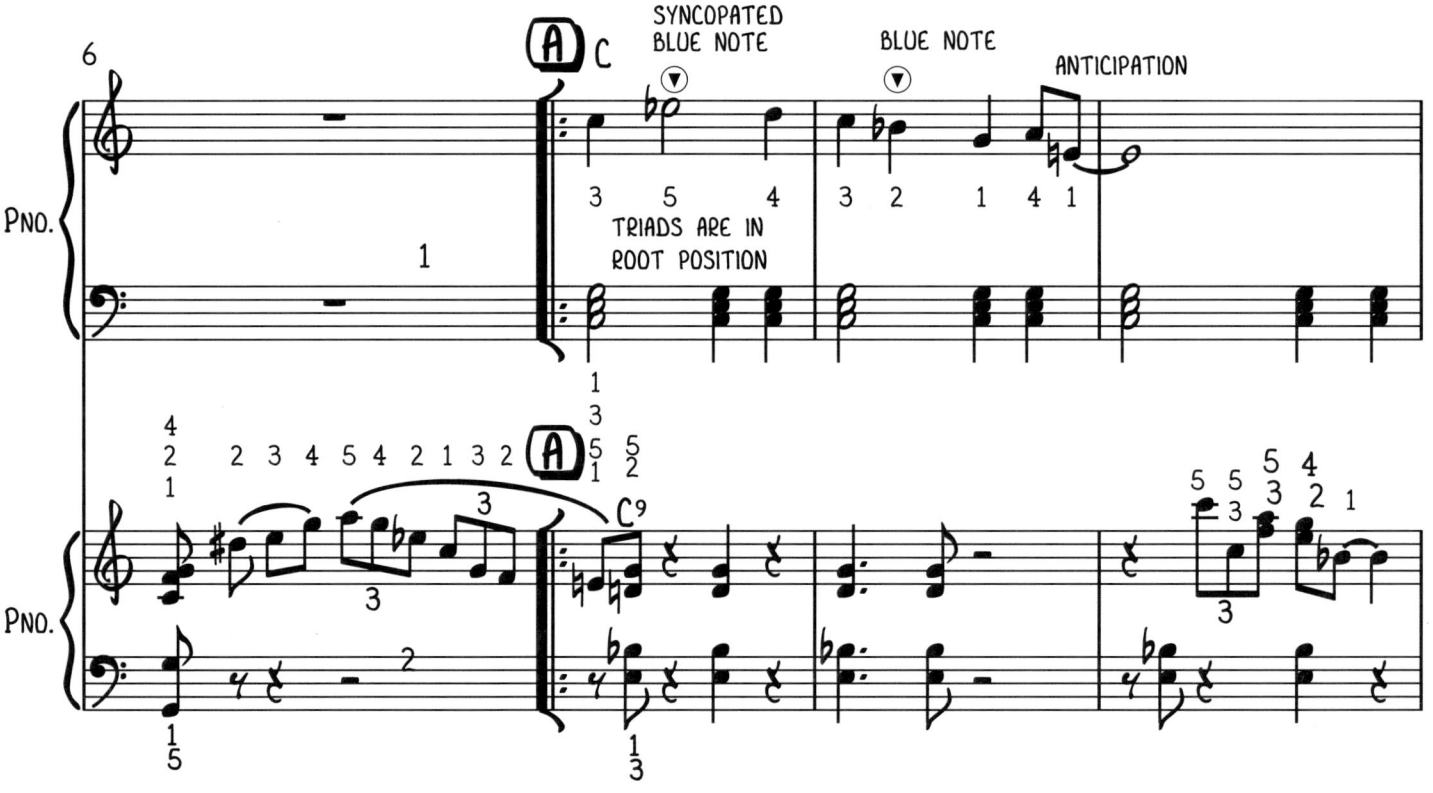

28

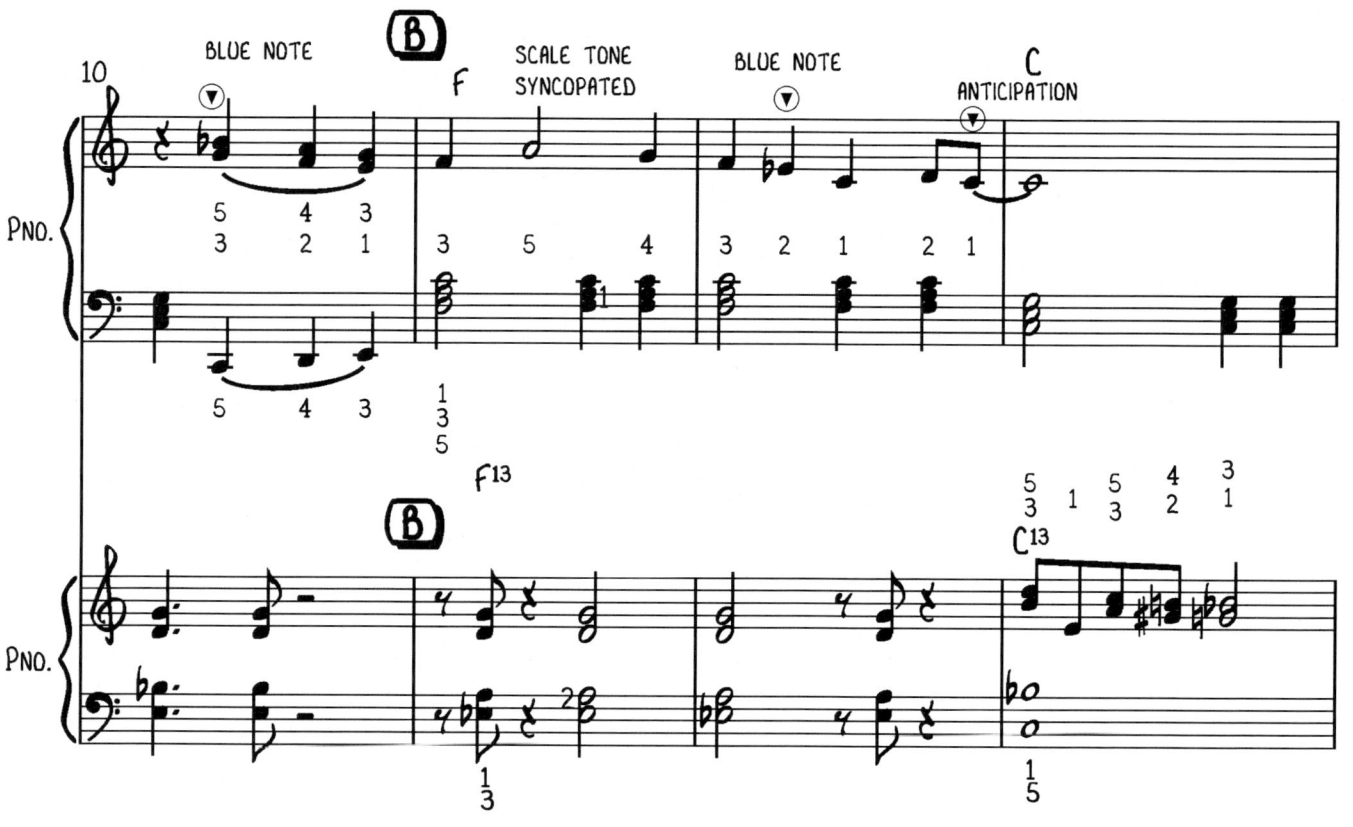
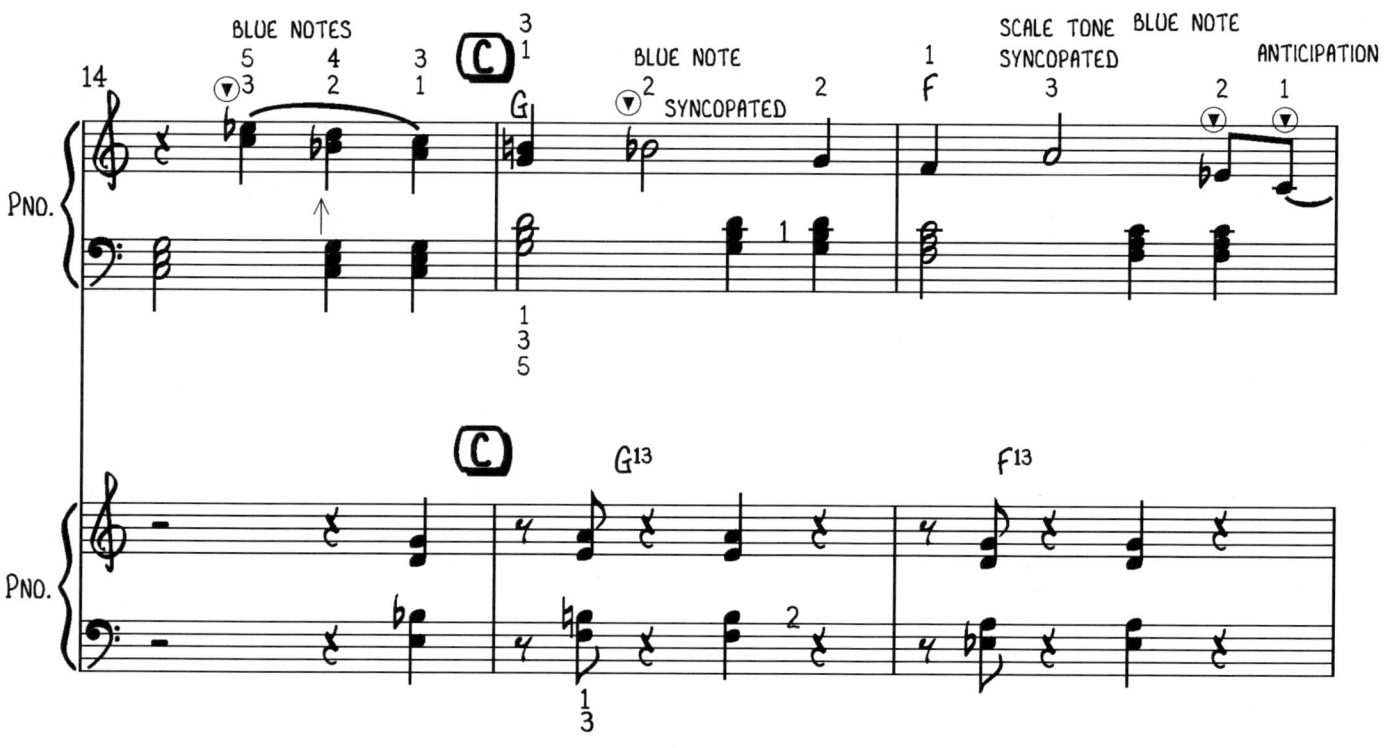

The next two examples show two aspects of syncopation: 1. Anticipation, and 2. Delay of the Beat. Both forms of syncopation are used regularly by jazz players.

**Example 14:  Syncopation: Anticipation**

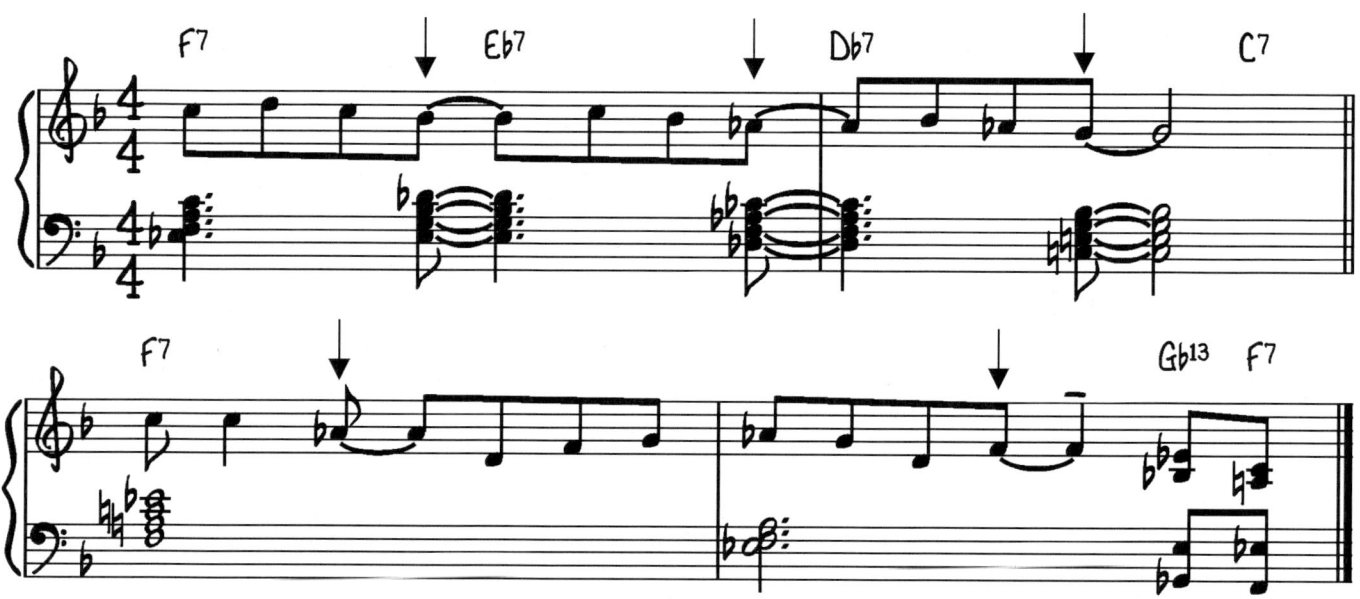

**Example 15:  Syncopation: Delay of the Beat**

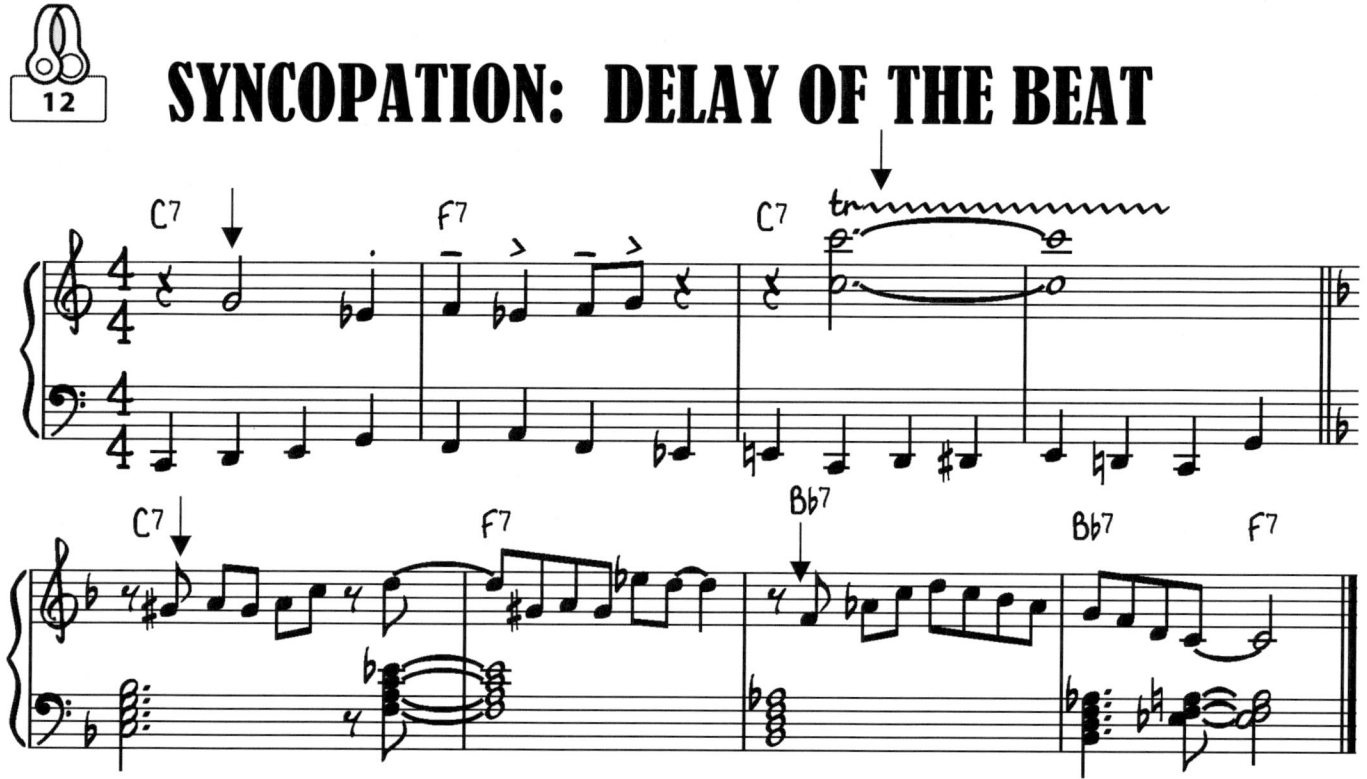

The next song introduces syncopation on beats three and four.

**Example 16: Strutting Horse Blues**

# STRUTTING HORSE BLUES

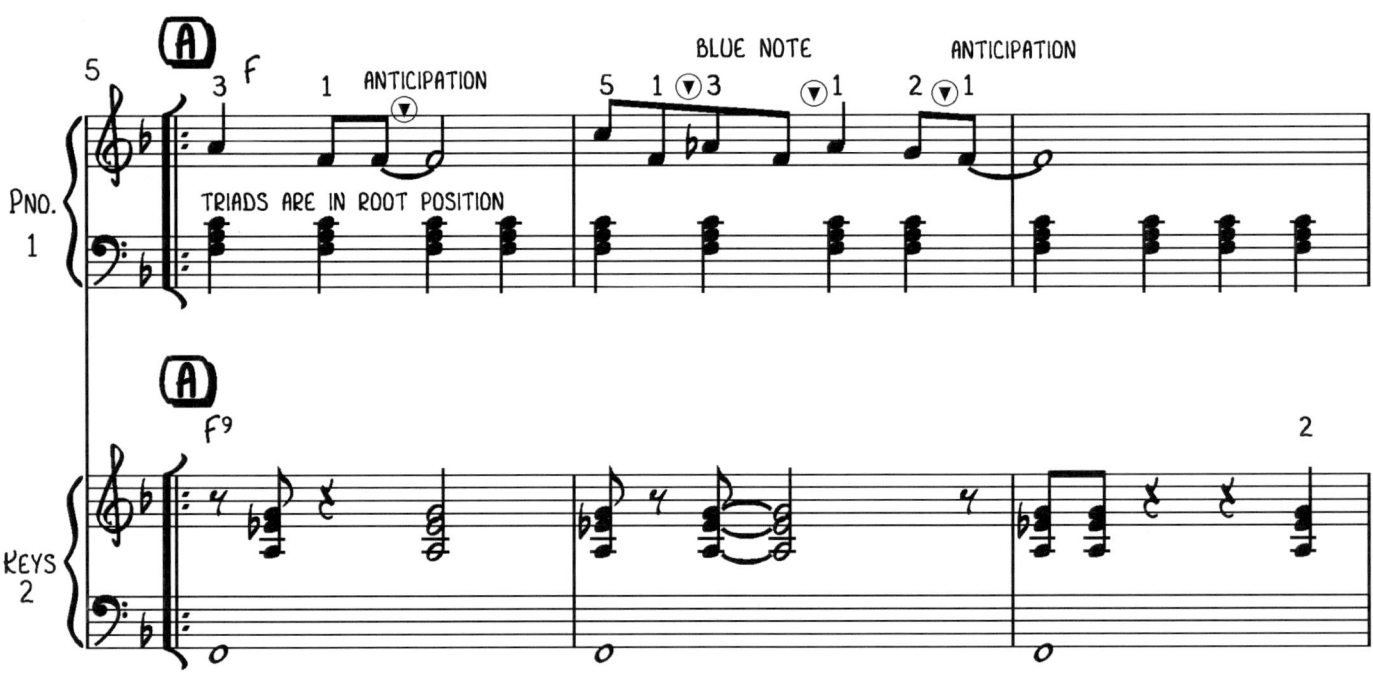

33

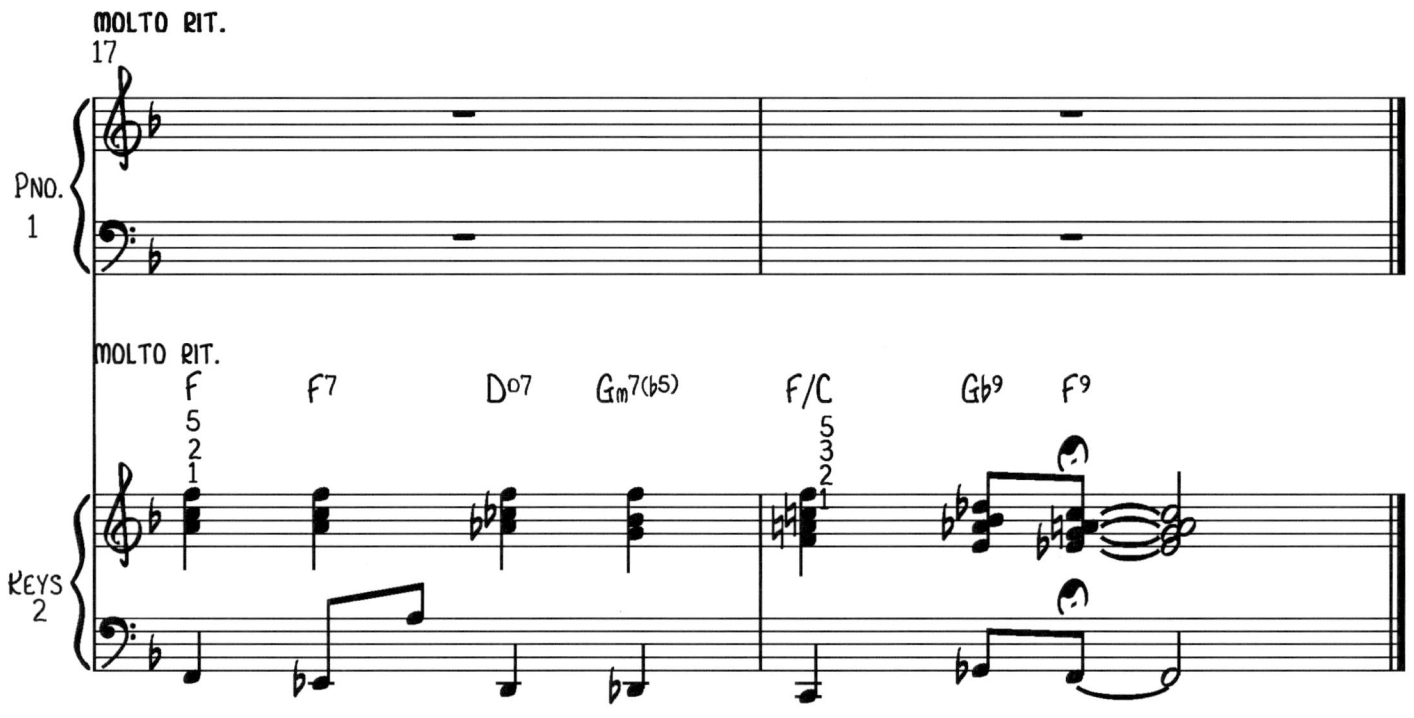

# III. BLUES MELODIES

Here is a simple blues melody harmonized a third lower. Notice that the double blue notes move in parallel motion. Note the use of contrary motion in the last measure. Play this piece in an easy, relaxed style.

**Example 17: A Simple Blues**

**Example 18: Blues Melody #2**

Notice the use of flatted sevenths, thirds and fifths in this example.

# Riffs

Blues melodies usually form simple motifs that are called "riffs." A riff is a short, repeated idea or motif that is played with the chord that creates energy and excitement. Riffs are particularly effective for instrumental backgrounds behind a soloist.

# Example 19: Blues Riffs

The next song is written in 12/8 meter and is to be played in a fast shuffle style. You are expected to play two notes with the right hand and one note with the left hand. Notice that the right hand is played with a lilting, uneven eighth-note feel.

The electric bass part sounds one octave lower than written.

*This page is left blank to avoid awkard page turns.*

**Example 20: Shuffle Blues**

# SHUFFLE BLUES

By Vince Corozine

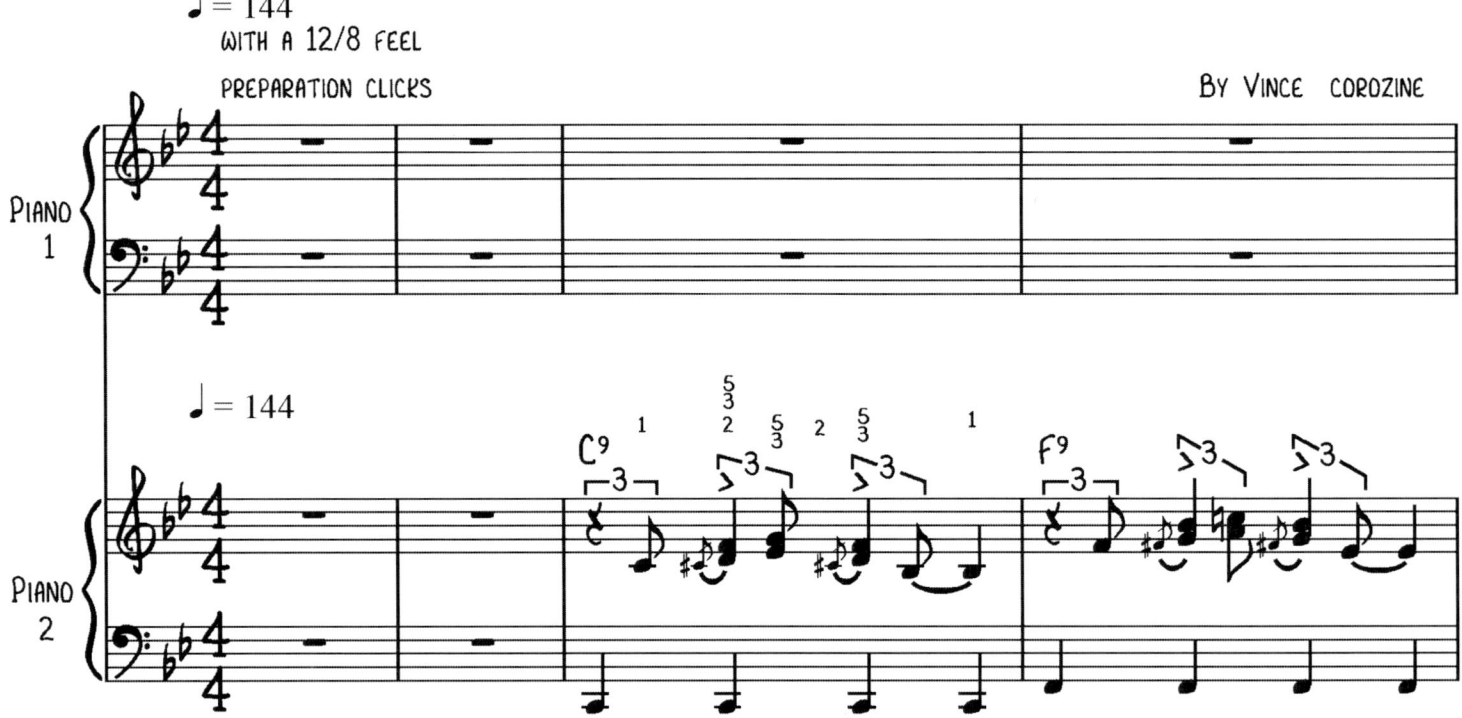

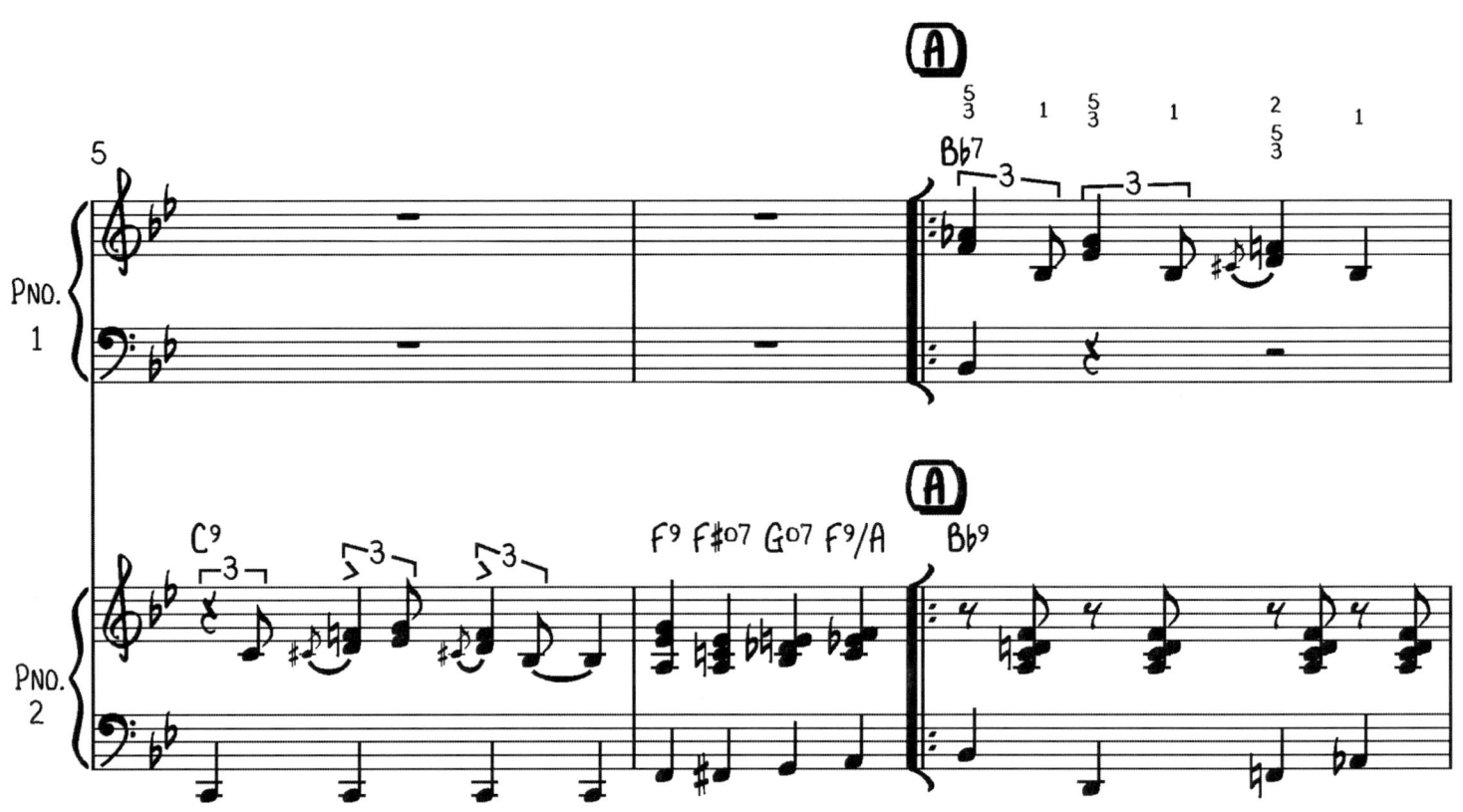

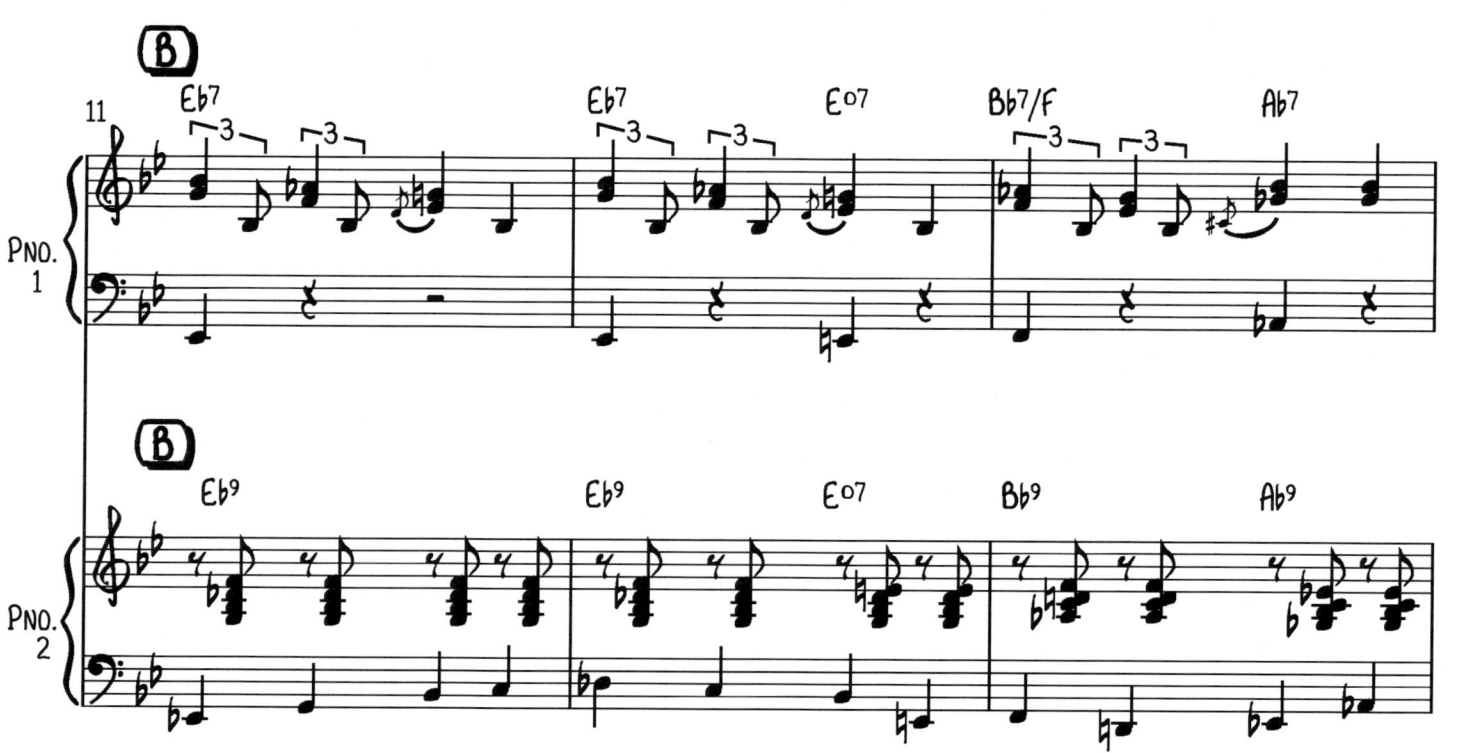

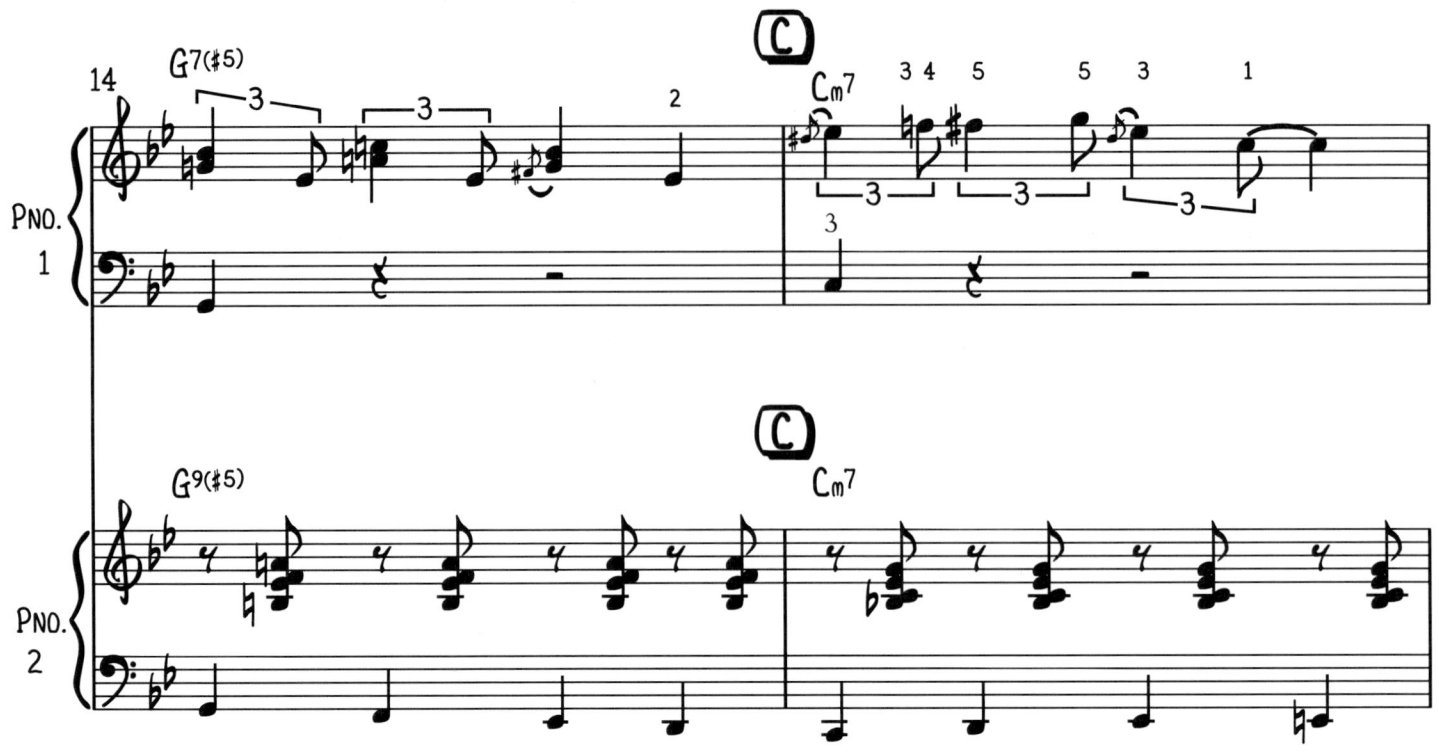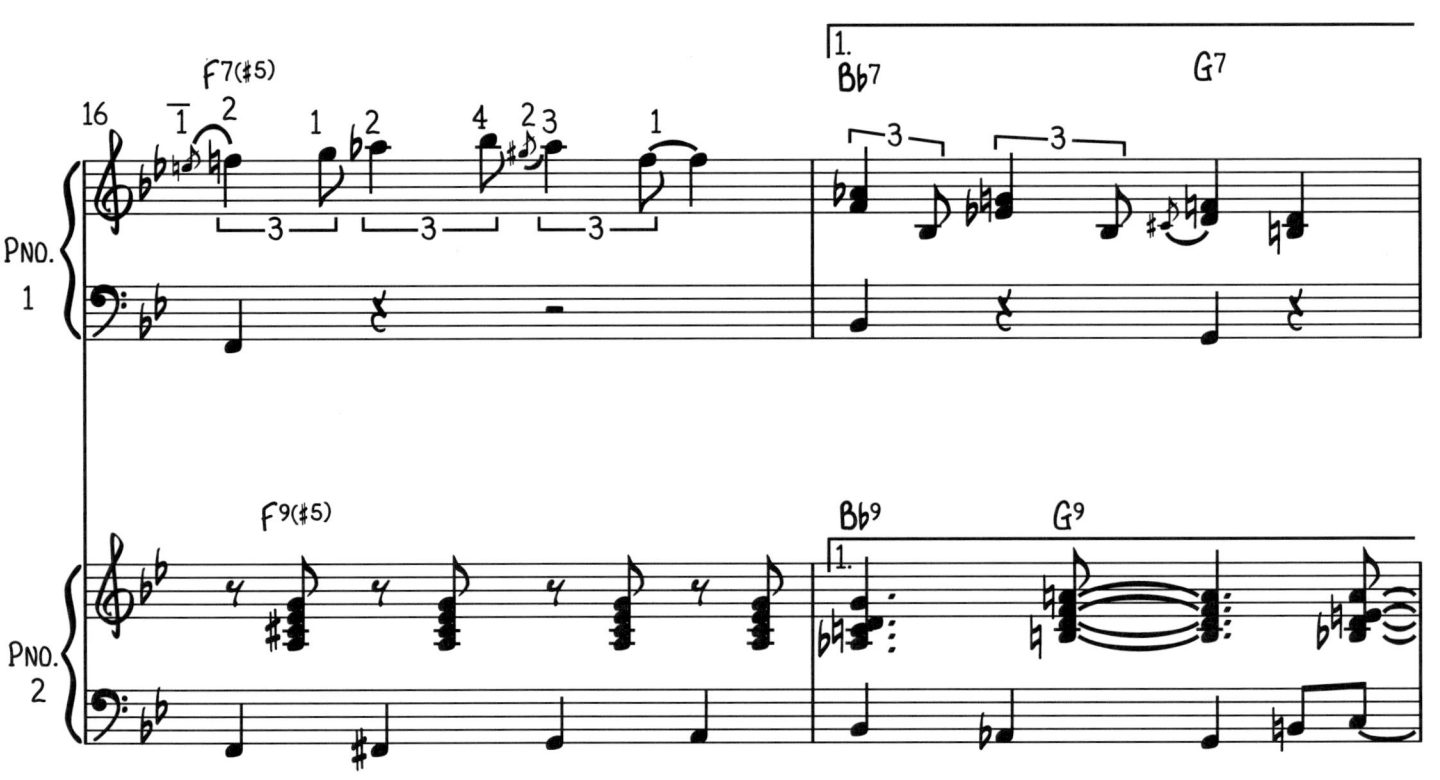

As mentioned previously, the call and response is the main idea of the blues form. The call states a question and creates tension (usually two measures), while the response produces an answer and resolves the tension, (usually two measures). Listen to the sound of the vibraphone and guitar as they play the "response" (answer) to the "call" played by the piano and bass.

**Example 21: Call and Response**

# CALL AND RESPONSE

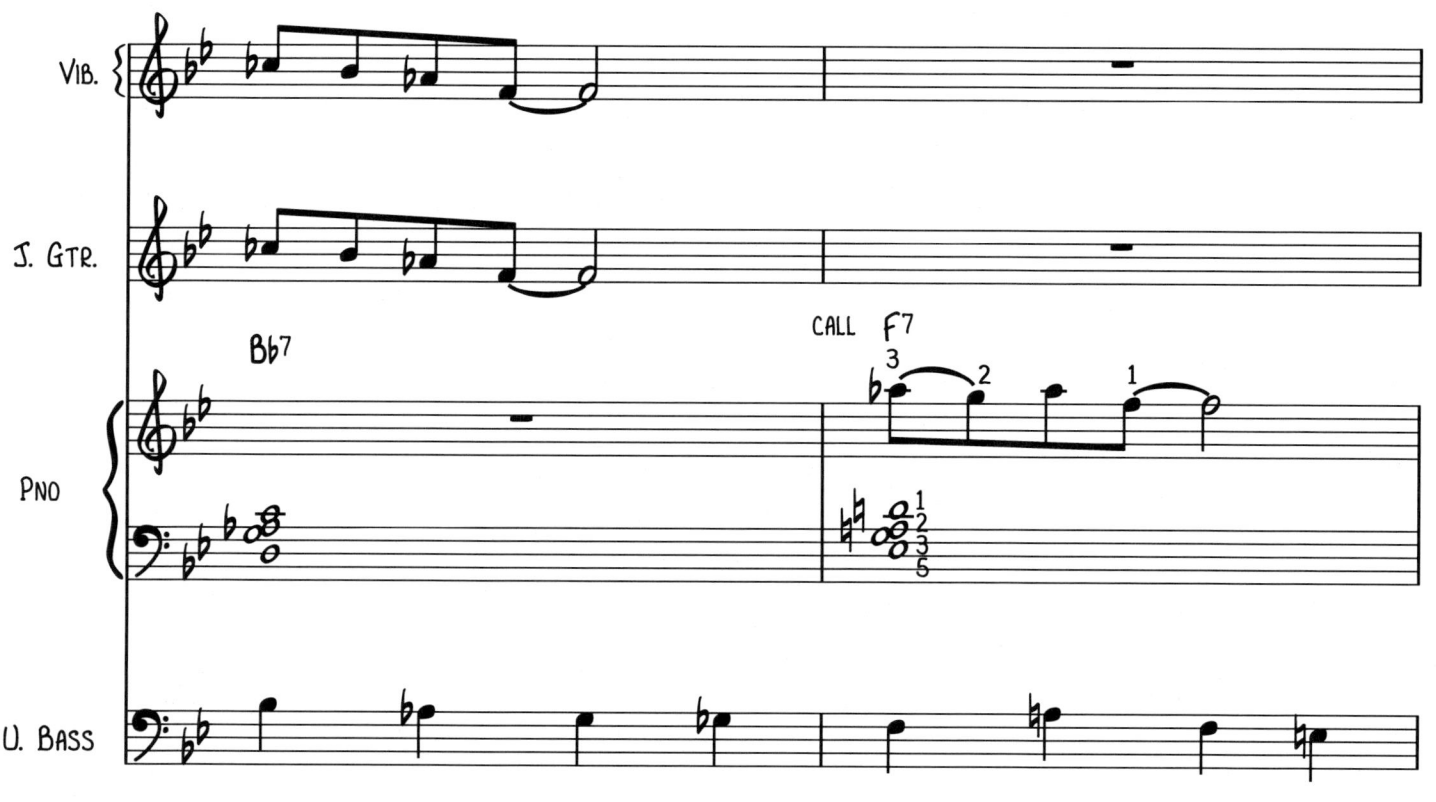

# IV. BASIC BLUES CHORDS

The blues is built upon a series of chords derived from the major scale. They are the tonic (I), subdominant (IV) and the dominant (V) chords. Most of the chords found in the blues are dominant seventh chords. These chords contain four notes as compared with triads that include only three notes. The dominant seventh adds a tone a minor third above the fifth of a major chord; this added note creates additional fullness and tension in the sound.

In the next example, all chords consist of three notes (triads) and are written in root position with the tonic as the lowest note.

**Example 22: Basic Chords Used in the Blues**

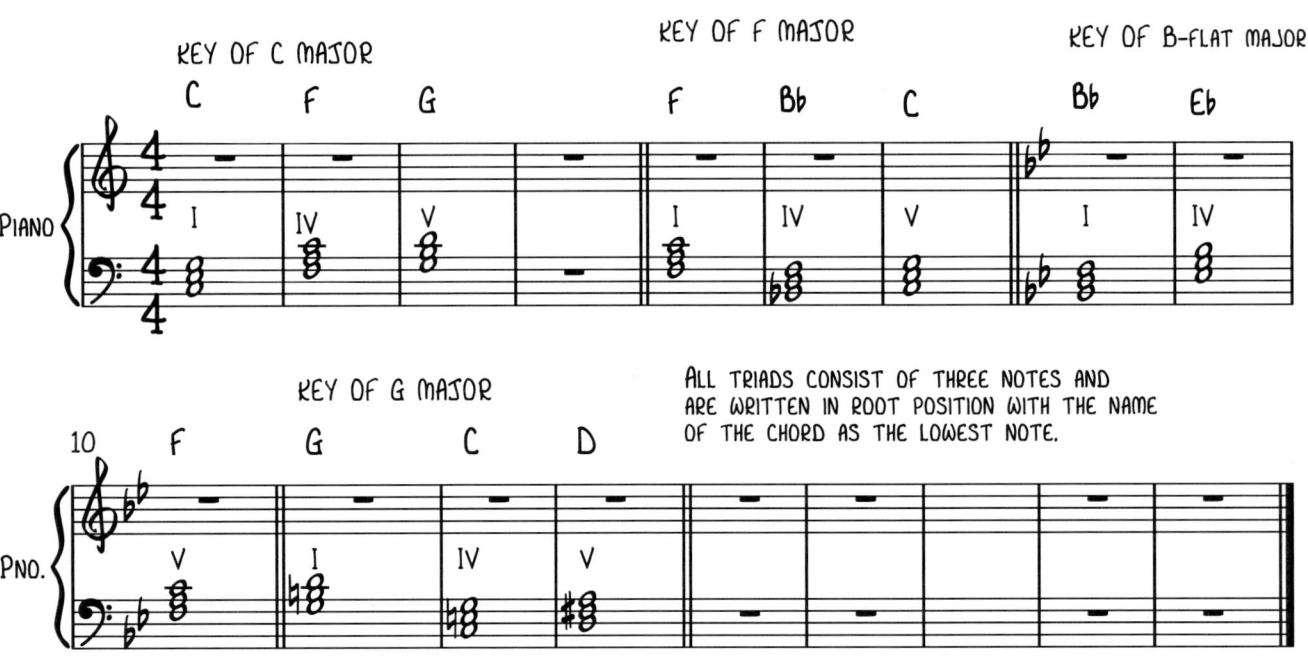

Chord symbols (F7, B♭7, C7) are used as a shorthand way of showing the possible voicings that can be played with the left hand or with both hands.
There are four main types of triads: major, minor, diminished, and augmented.

**Example 23: Four Types of Triads**

There are also five types of seventh chords: major 7, minor 7, half-diminished 7, (minor 7♭5) diminished 7, and dominant 7. The dominant seventh is the most commonly used chord in the blues.

**Example 24: Five Types of Seventh Chords**

## V. CHORD INVERSIONS

Chords may be played in various position or *inversions*. Inversions are a rearrangement of the tones in a chord to allow for a smoother progression of notes with a minimum of hand movement between chords.

Until now, you have been playing chords that are in root position (root, third and 5th). By moving to the next nearest notes the fingers will move less often and the sound will be smoother and as a result, easier to play. Inversions minimize hand movement. This helps to avoid unnecessary, awkward interval skips from one chord to another.

The next song uses chord inversions in the left hand. When a chord is voiced for a keyboard it is the lowest note that determines the inversion. When the number 6 is placed under a chord, it means that the third of the chord is the lowest note and is referred to as the *first inversion*. When a 6/4 is placed under a chord, it means that the fifth of the chord is in the lowest note, and is referred to as the *second inversion*.

**Example 25:  Chord Inversions**

# CHORD INVERSIONS

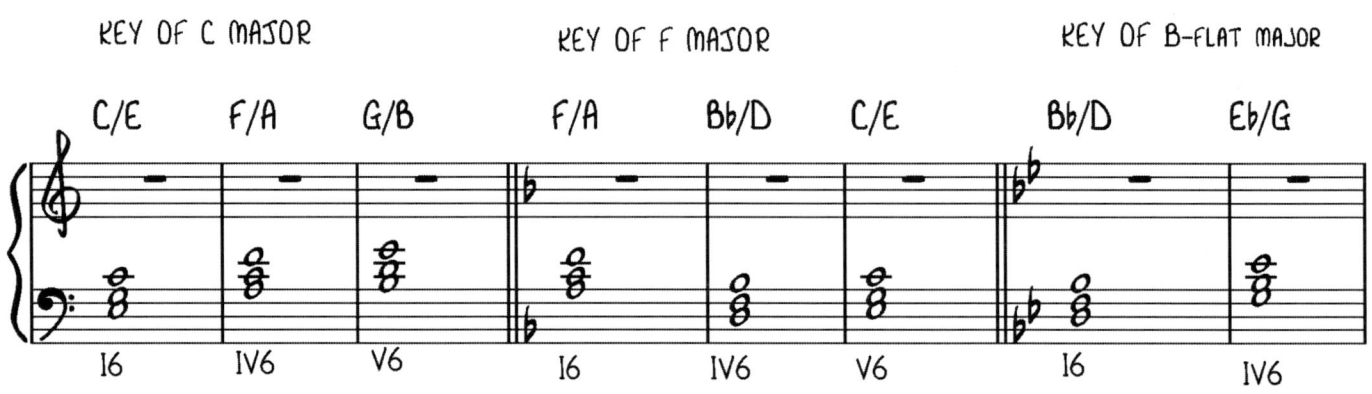

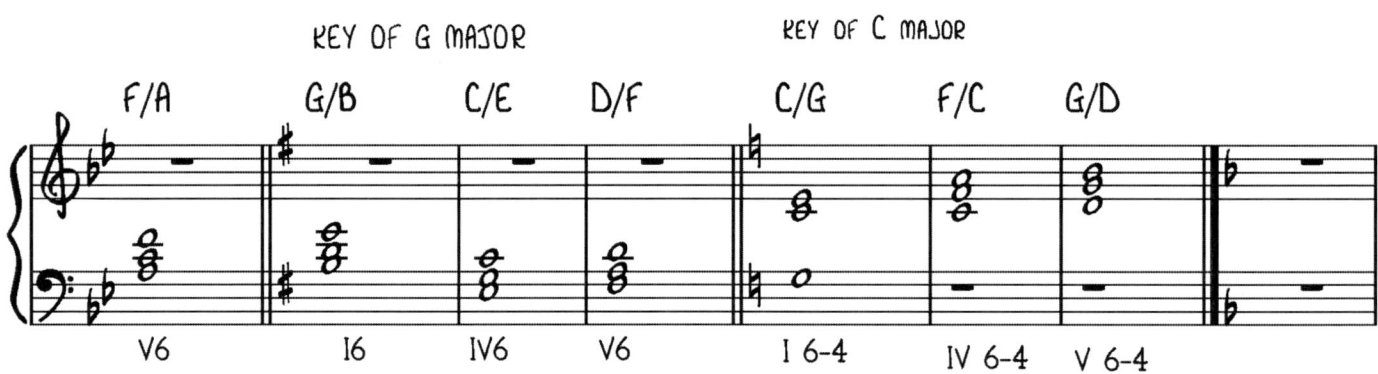

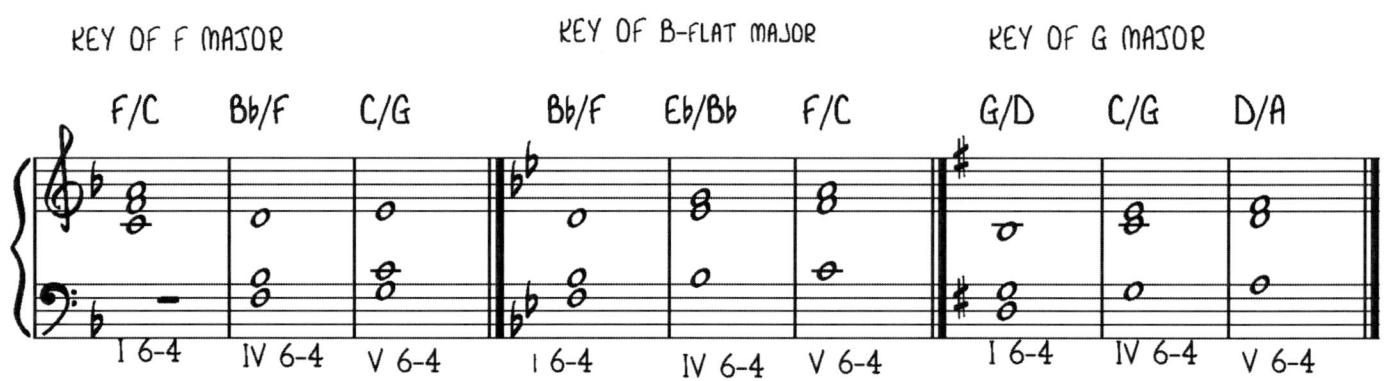

**Example 26:** Nervous Monkey Blues

The following example contains blue notes, grace notes and anticipation of the beat.

# NERVOUS MONKEY BLUES

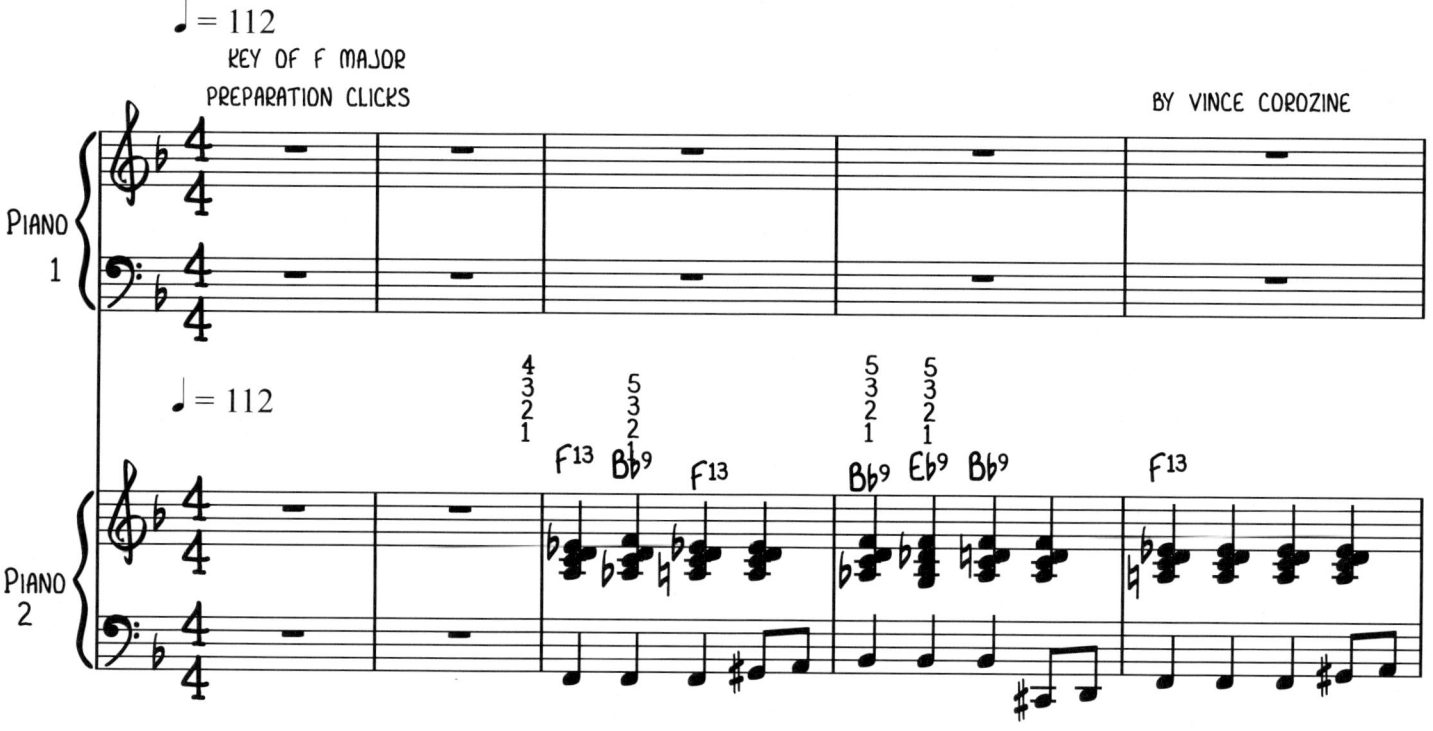

**Example 27:** *Sneaky Cat Blues*

# SNEAKY CAT BLUES

New Orleans staight 8ths
preparation clicks

By Vince Corozine

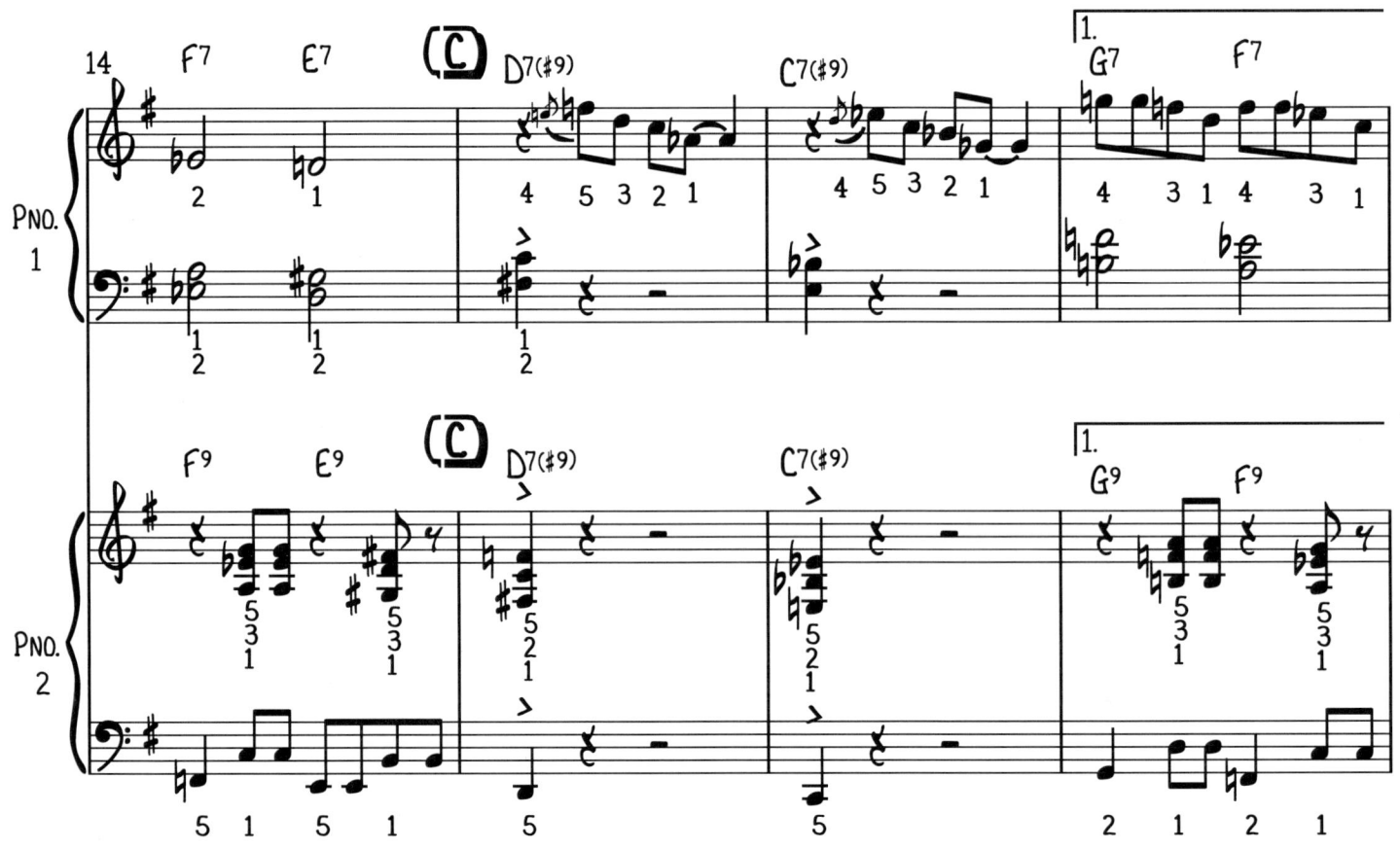

When you are playing piano (or guitar) with a bass player, you do not have to include the root of the chord in your playing. The bass player will play the roots of the chords, particularly on the first beat of a measure.

When playing up-tempo songs, do not use the sustain pedal. It is better if the chords do not run into one another. When playing slower songs (ballads) the sustain pedal may be used discriminately.

## SLASH CHORDS

Inversions are often indicated by the use of "slash" chord symbols such as C/D which means that you are to play a C major triad in the right hand over a D bass note in the left hand. Notice that the right hand is voiced in 6/4 inversion with the fifth on the bottom. Chords sound more resonant when voiced in 6/4 position. Slash chords describe specific combinations of upper triads over a bass note other than the root.

**Example 28: Slash Chords**

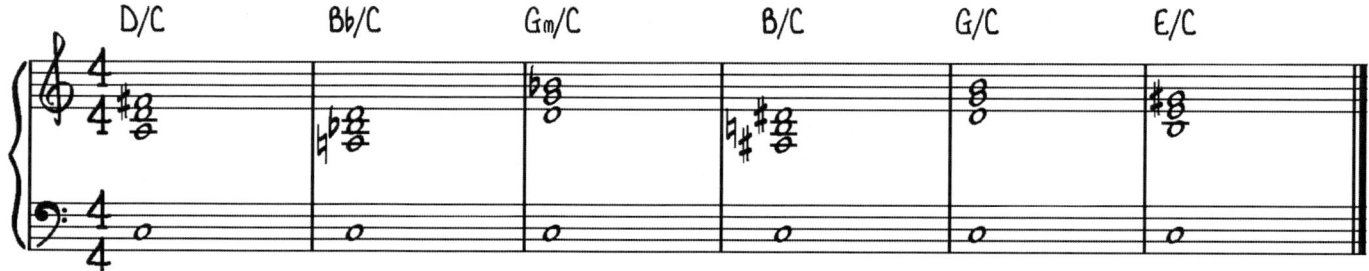

## VI. LEFT-HAND PATTERNS

There are four basic left-hand patterns used for playing the blues.

### Boogie Woogie (single-note pattern)

The early jazz players called it, "Playing eight to the bar."

**Example 29: Boogie Woogie Single-Note Pattern**

# BOOGIE WOOGIE SINGLE-NOTE PATTERN

Boogie Woogie or "Barrel House Blues" is an exciting percussive rhythm that propels the blues along and creates a strong rhythmic background. Boogie Woogie uses mostly fast tempos with driving left-hand percussive patterns.

This song should be performed with a straight eighth-note feel.

Famous Boogie-Woogie pianists include: Albert Ammons, Pete Johnson, Meade Lux Lewis, and Cow-Cow Davenport.

In the next example, notice the boogie-woogie pattern in the second piano part. Let the feeling of continuous eighth notes lead you in your playing of "Oogie Boogie Woogie".

Example 30: Oogie Boogie Woogie

# OOGIE BOOGIE WOOGIE

♩ = 120
STRAIGHT EIGHTH-NOTE BOOGIE STYLE

BY VINCE COROZINE

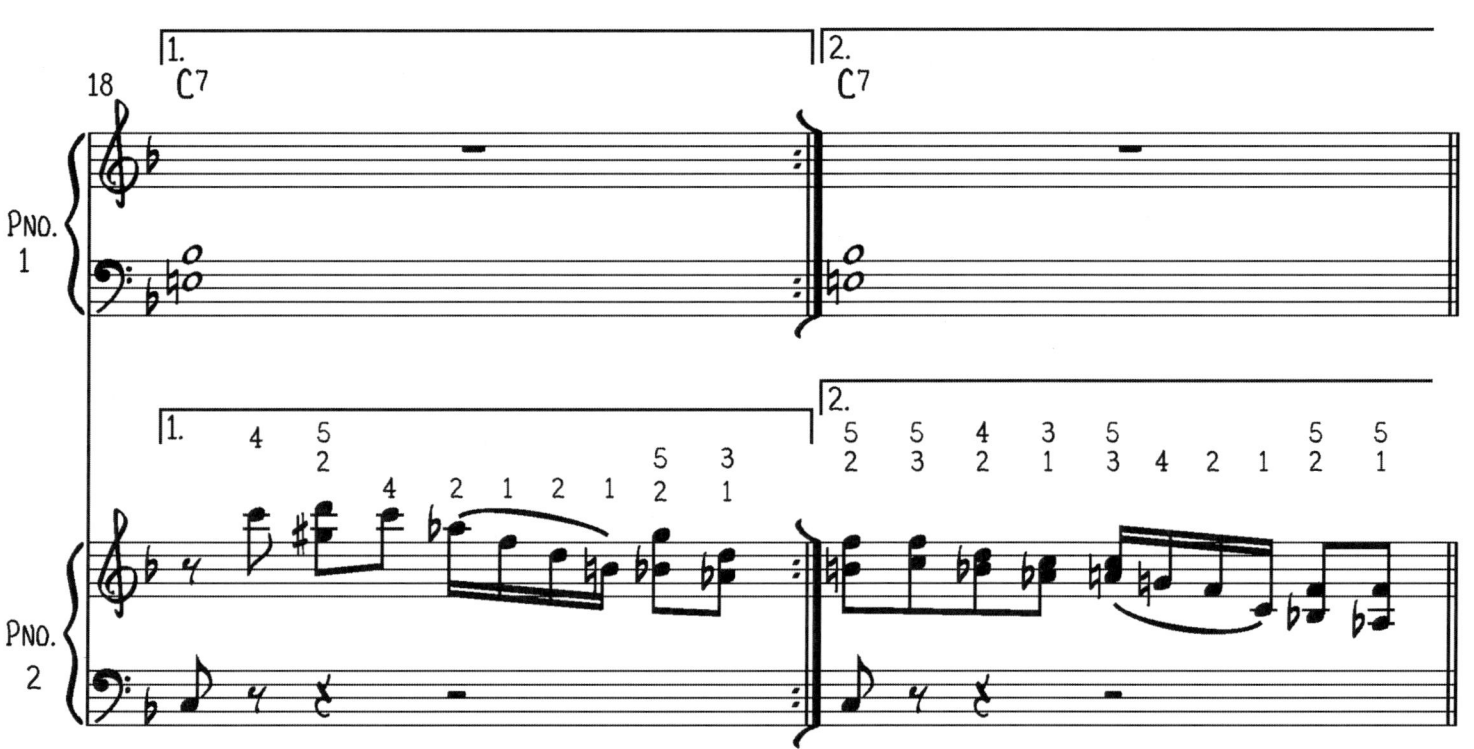

**Example 31:** Boogie Woogie (two-note pattern)

# BOOGIE WOOGIE: TWO-NOTE PATTERN

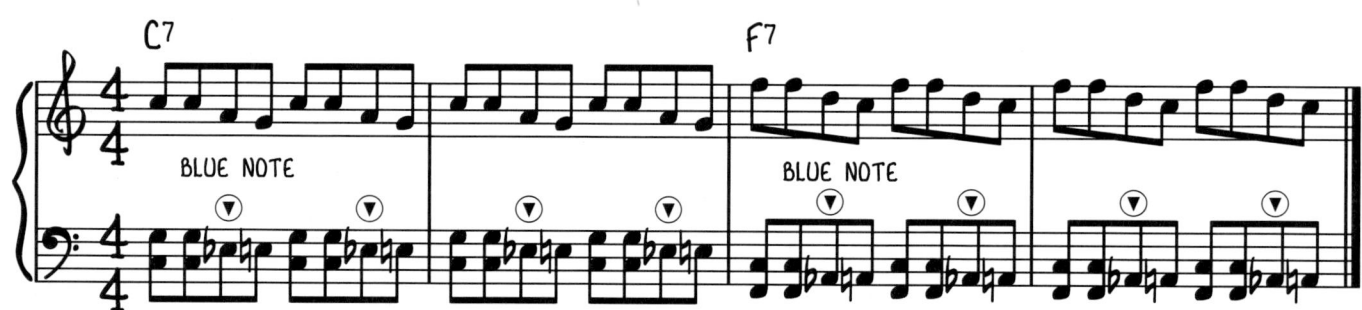

Next, we will add a melody to the two-note boogie-woogie pattern. The lowered thirds in each measure are marked with a triangle in a circle. Notice how the last measure moves in contrary motion.

**Example 32:** Another Boogie Woogie

# ANOTHER BOOGIE WOOGIE

♩ = 142

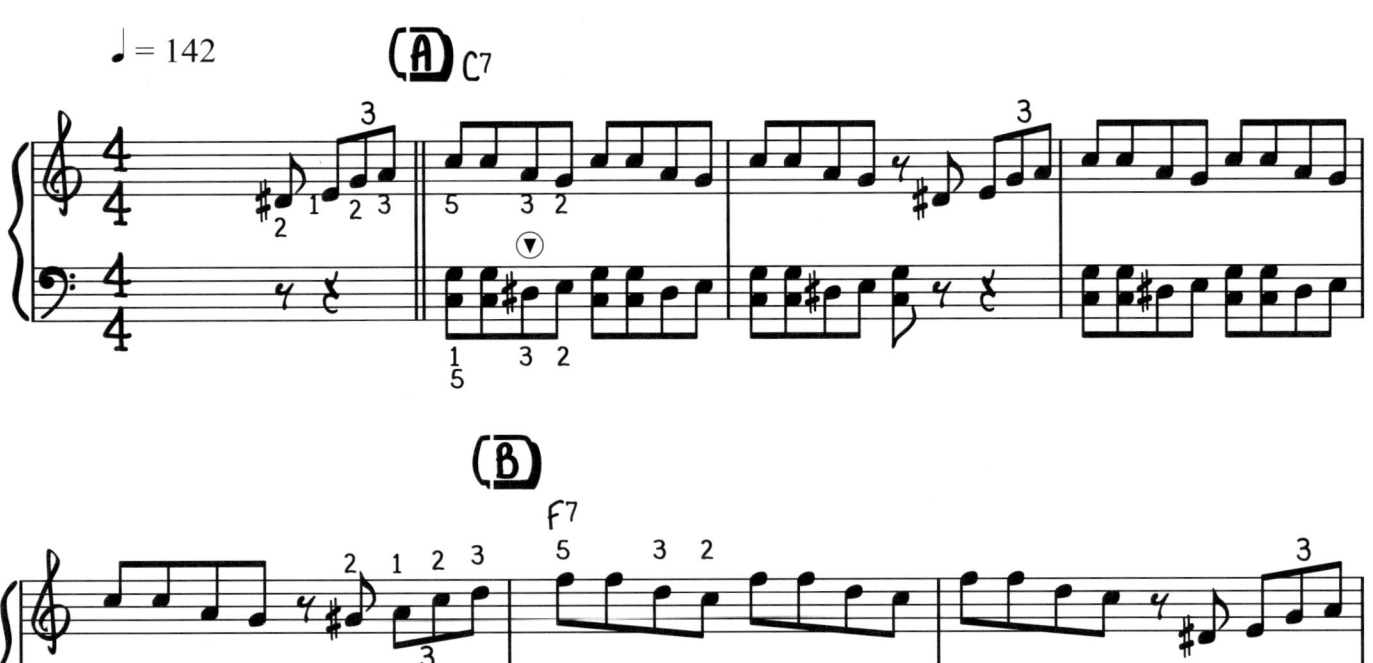

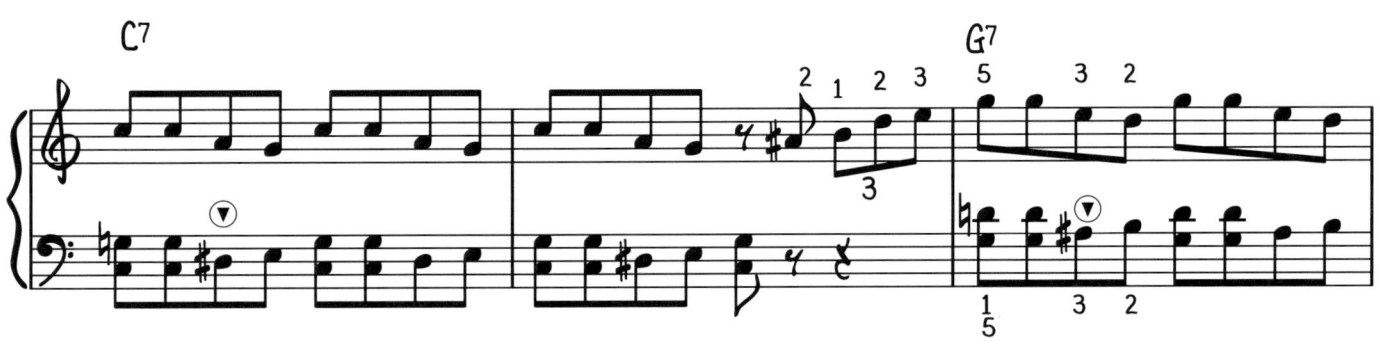

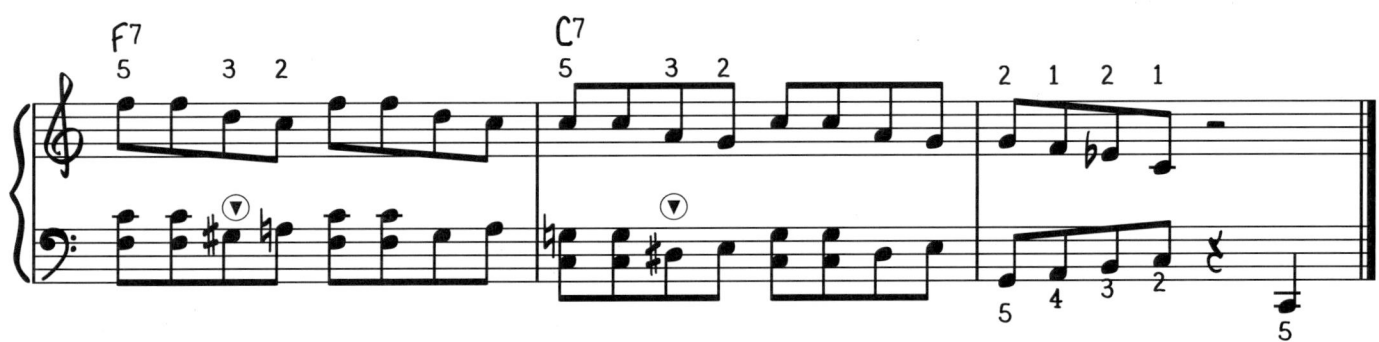

61

**B. Walking Bass**

Walking bass refers to a series of quarter notes played by the left hand on each beat of the measure, with the root, 3rd and 7th of the chord played in the bass line, with whole and half-step approach tones leading to these important chord tones. This bass device outlines the chord progression and provides melodic movement and interest. This is an alternative to playing full chords all the time. Most of the time the walking bass outlines the notes found in the blues scale.

Notice that the the half steps used to connect the chord third to the fifth (3, 4, ♯4, 5 as in measure 9), or the seventh to the fifth (♭7, 6, ♭6, 5 as in measure 3). (Remember that the bass part sounds an octave lower than written, when played by an upright or electric bass).

**Example 33: Walking Bass**

In the next song, listen for the walking bass part in the accompaniment and the syncopated anticipation pattern in most of the measures.

**Example 34: Running Rabbit Blues**

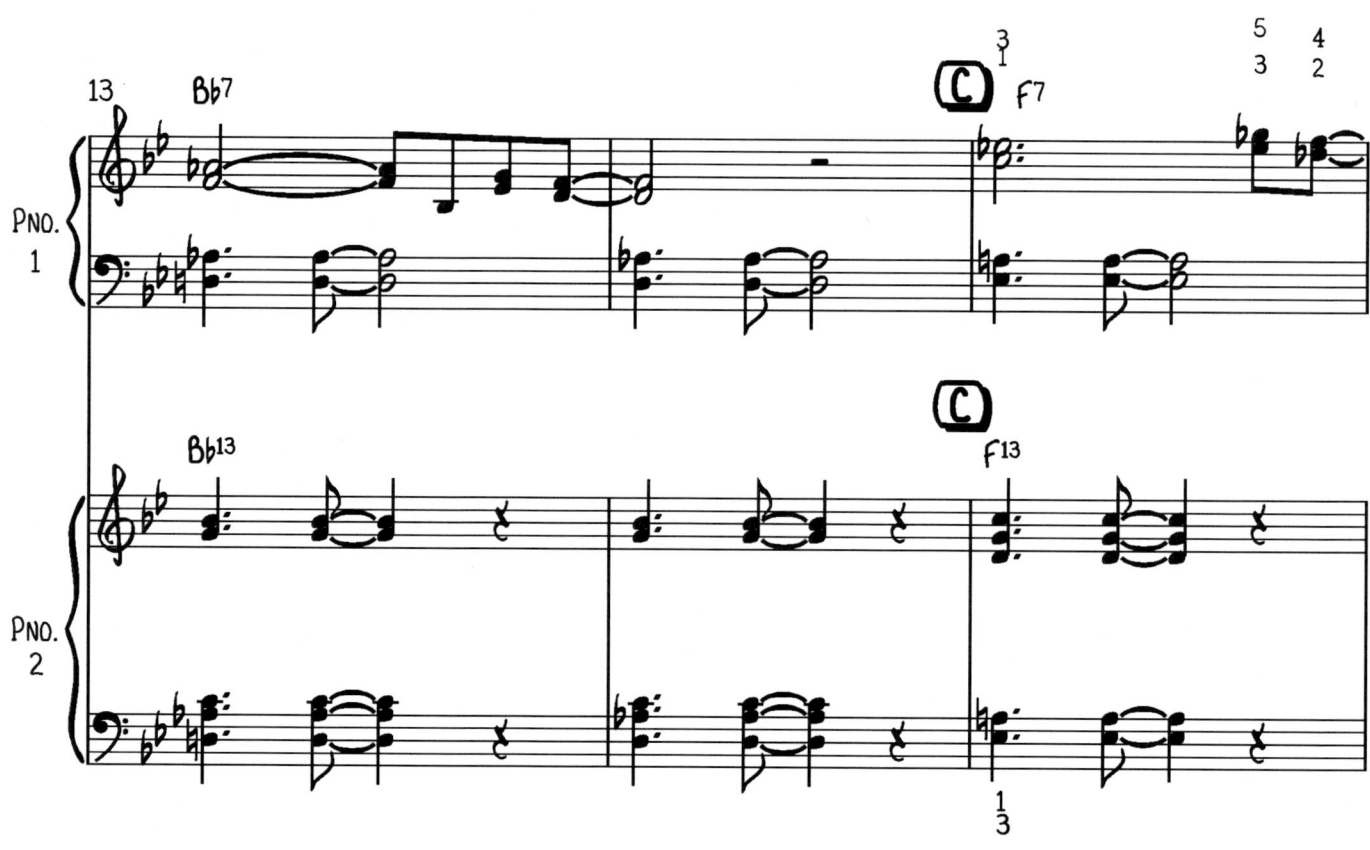

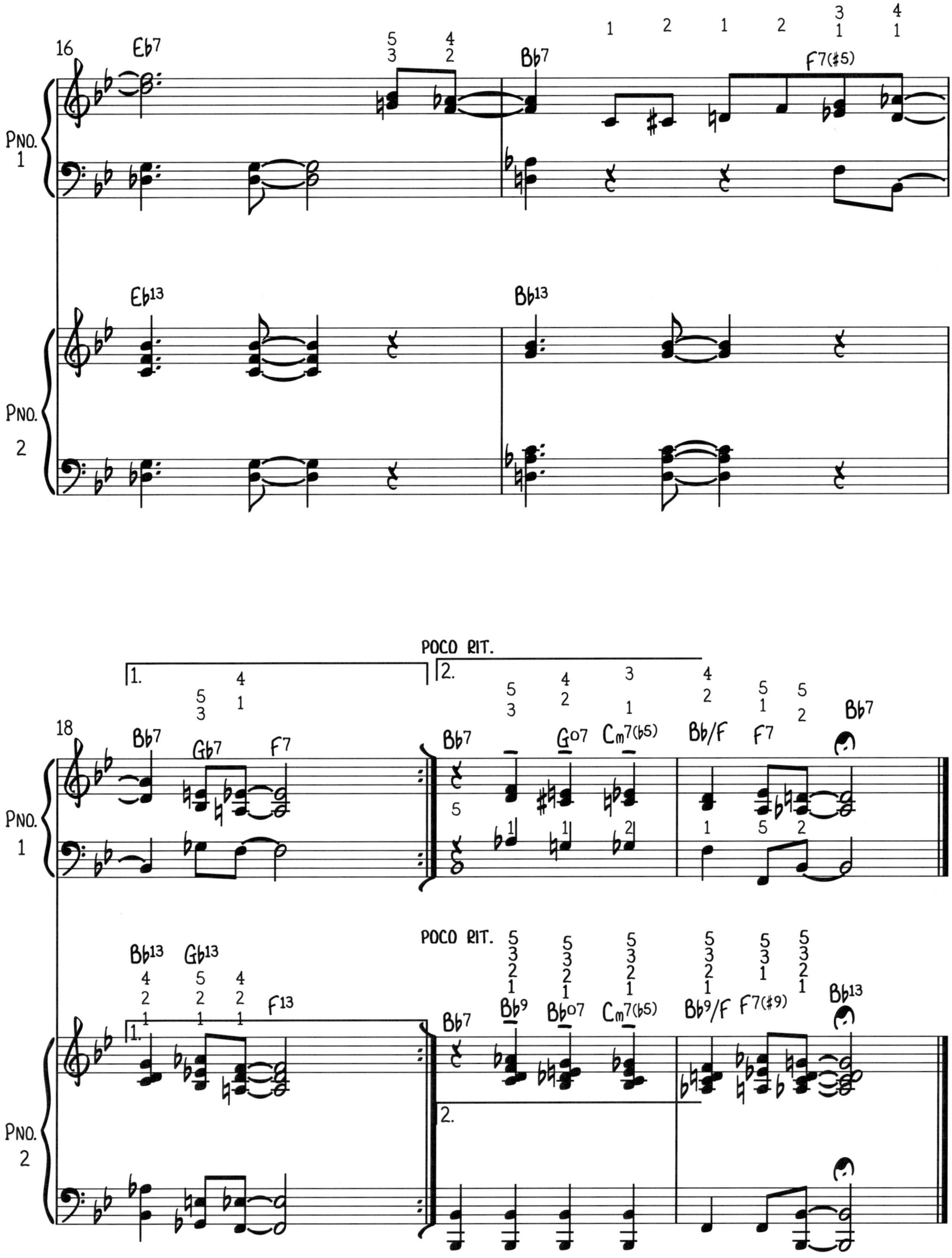
16
Eb7
Bb7
F7(#5)
PNO. 1
Eb13
Bb13
PNO. 2
POCO RIT.
1.
2.
18
Bb7
Gb7
F7
G○7
Cm7(b5)
Bb/F
F7
Bb7
POCO RIT.
Bb13
Gb13
F13
Bb9
Bb○7
Bb9/F
F7(#9)

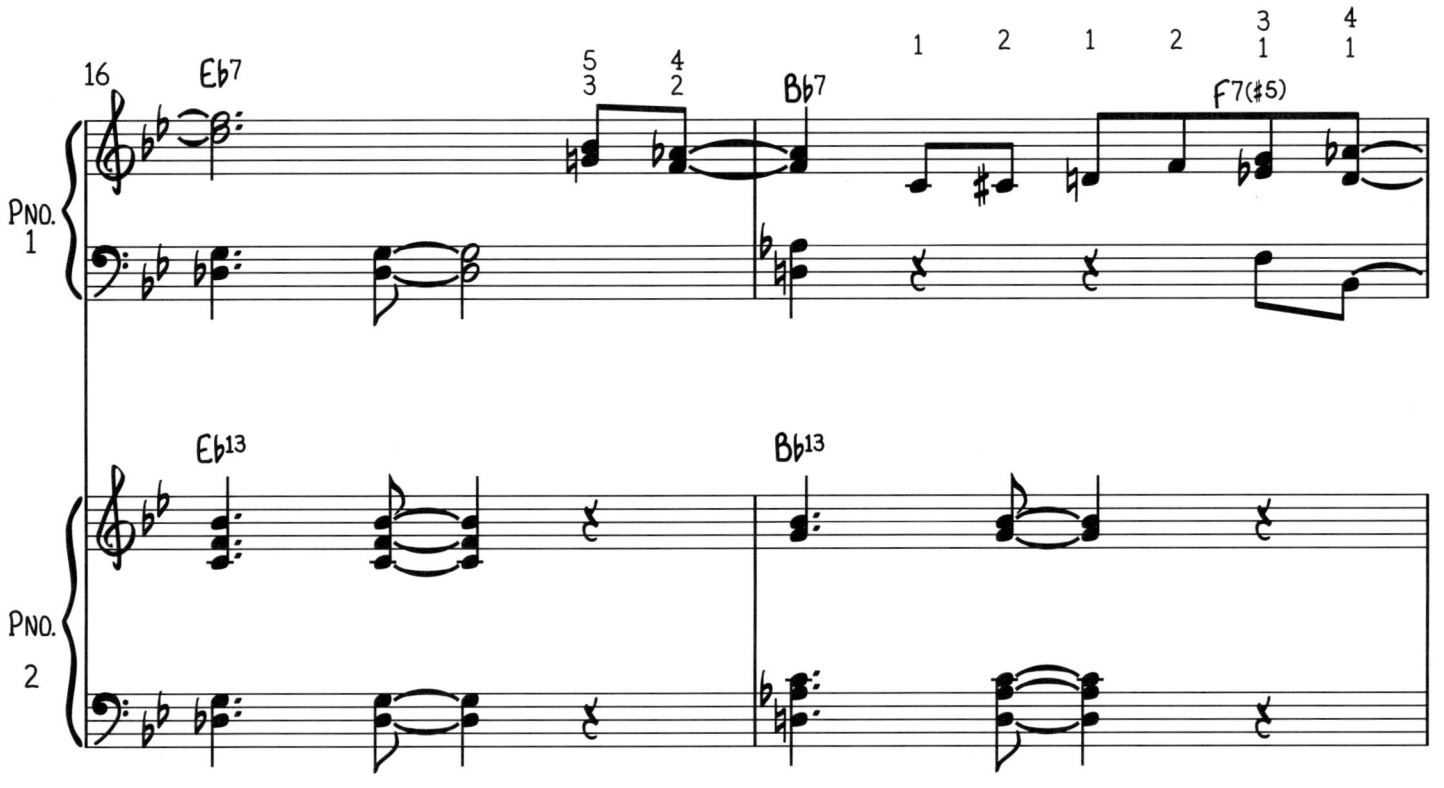

### C. Shell (Guide-Tone) Voicings

"Shell" or open voicings, where some notes of the chord are omitted, create contrast through the use of a lighter and more open sound. These voicings are important tools for the jazz pianist to master. For variety, you can sometimes put the third of a chord on the bottom, or use the seventh of the chord on the bottom. The third and seventh of a chord are considered to be important "color" tones, and are often referred to as *guide tones*.

The movement from third to seventh, or seventh to third voicing can be used in either the right or left hand. Most shell voicings simulate the sound of dominant seventh chords, which sound fuller than triads. In the next example, observe the close voice-leading; the notes move by half-steps from one chord to the next.

**Example 35: Shell Voicings**

The bassist may play the written note (above) or may supply the root along with what is played by the keyboard player.

Notice the "stop tempo" in the next song and the use of open "shell" voicings in the left hand. Play this with a straight-eighth note feel. This song has a 1950s Rock and Roll feel.

**Example 36:** Barrel Boogie Blues

# BARREL BOOGIE BLUES

By Vince Corozine

67

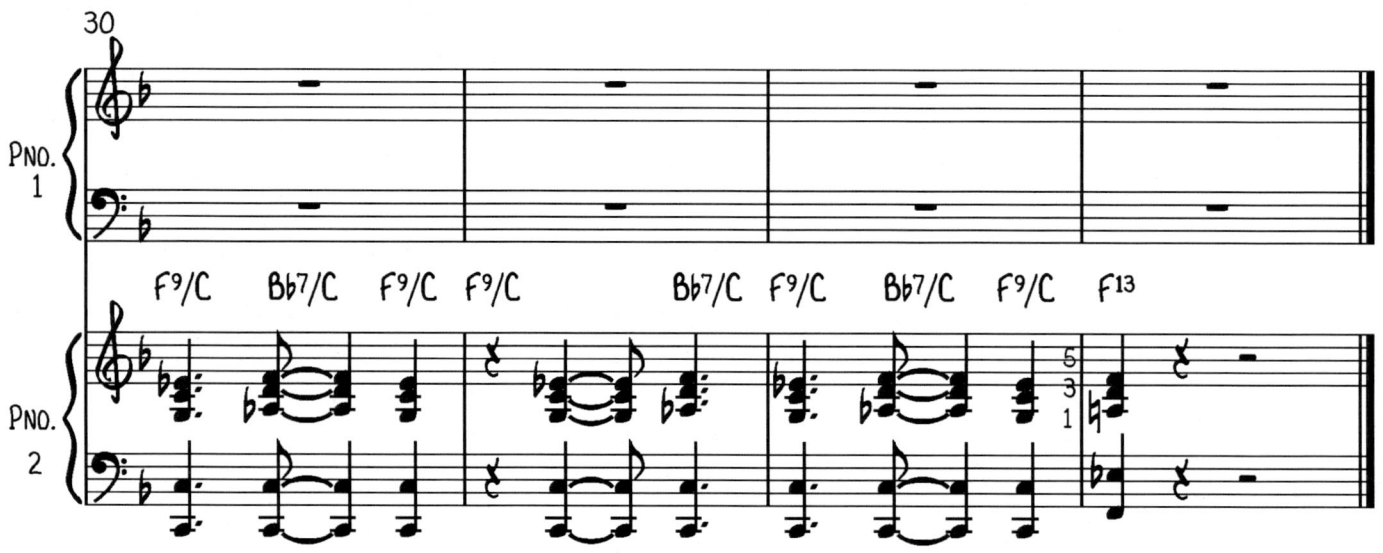

### D. Stride Piano Playing

Most early jazz pianists played in a stride style: a style featuring a bass pattern of single bass notes on the first and third beats and chords on the second and fourth. The left hand "strides" back and forth between bass notes and chords. In this style of playing you must get your fingers to move quickly and "dance over the keys." Famous stride pianists include: Teddy Wilson, Fats Waller, Art Tatum, Dick Hyman, Theolonius Monk, and Mary Lou Williams.

**Example 37:** Stride Piano Playing

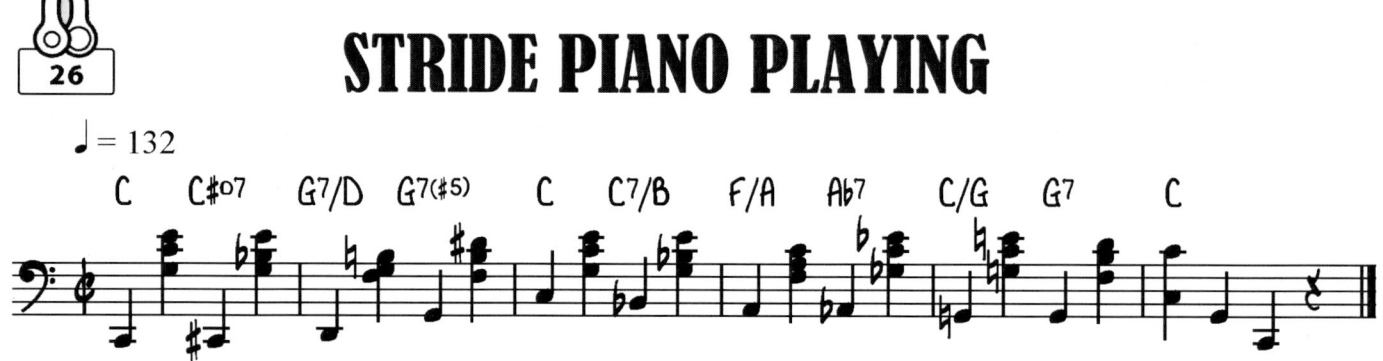

# VII. RHYTHMIC INTERPRETATION

Most blues songs are played with a jazz "swing" feel as opposed to a straight-eighth rock feel. Playing with a swing feel means that one interprets the notes in a 12/8 pattern rather than in a 4/4 pattern. Two eighth notes are played as modified triplets and are not evenly played.

**Example 38: Straight Eighths and Swing Eighths**

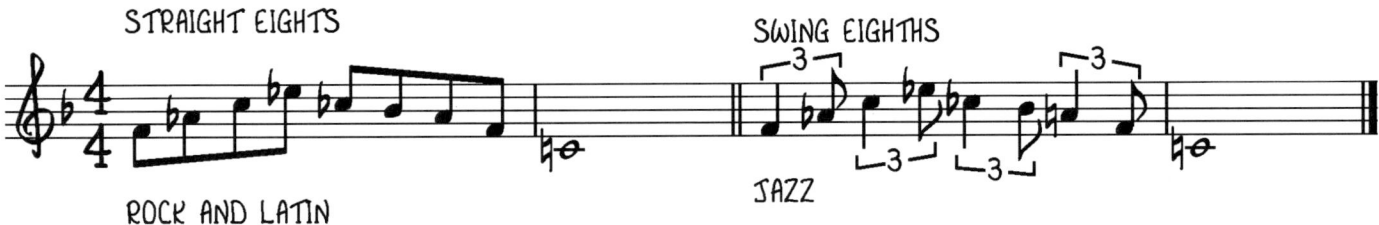

The next song, a slow rock ballad, with a 12/8 feel, has an active bass part containing lots of chromatic notes.

**Example 40: Petrified Parrot Blues**

# PETRIFIED PARROT BLUES

BY VINCE COROZINE

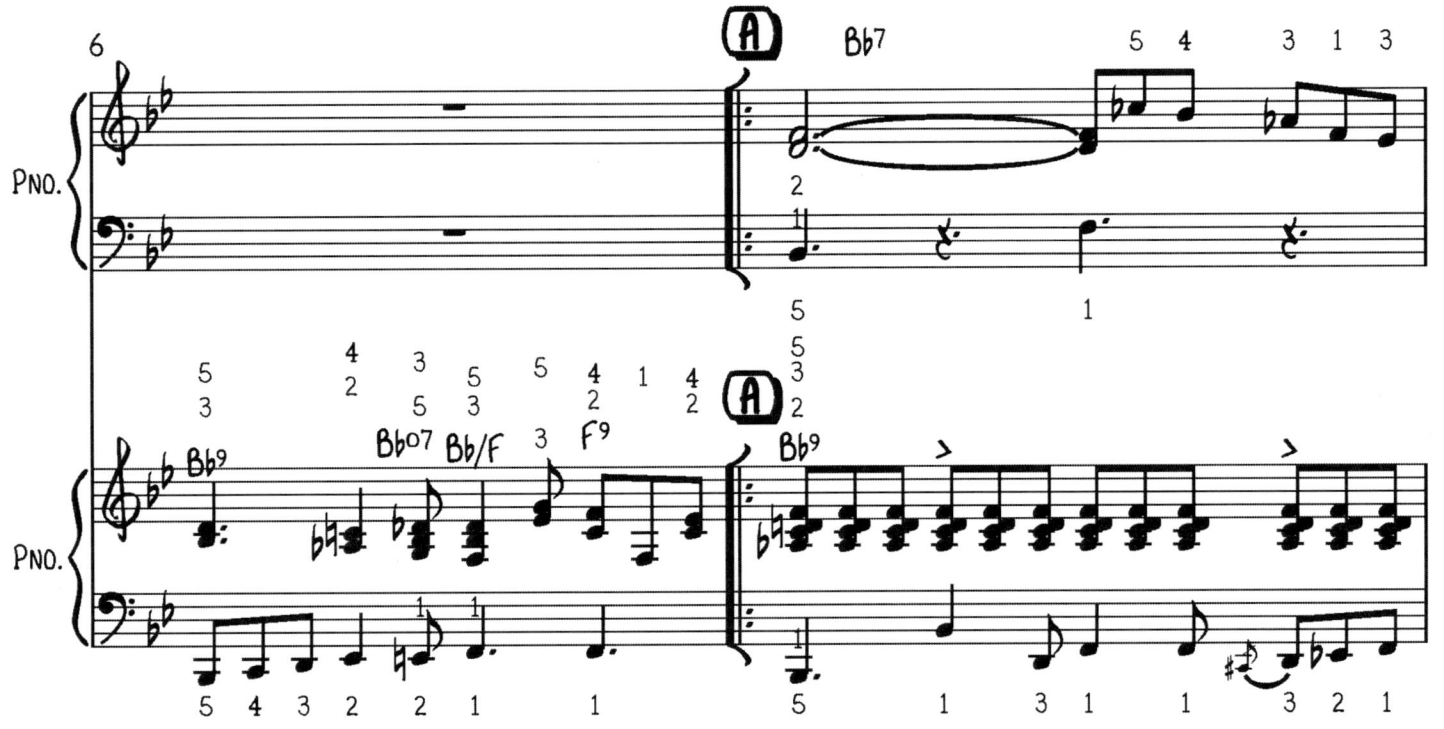

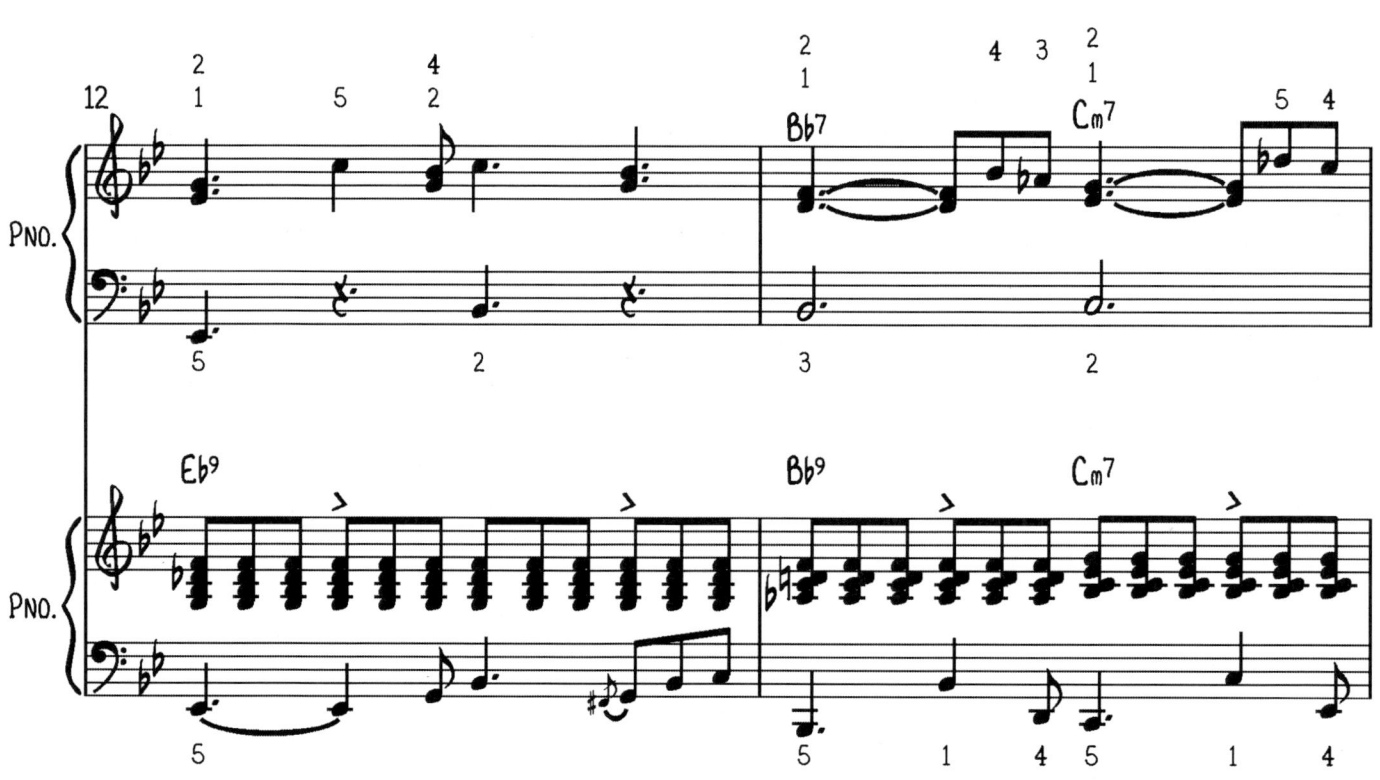

74

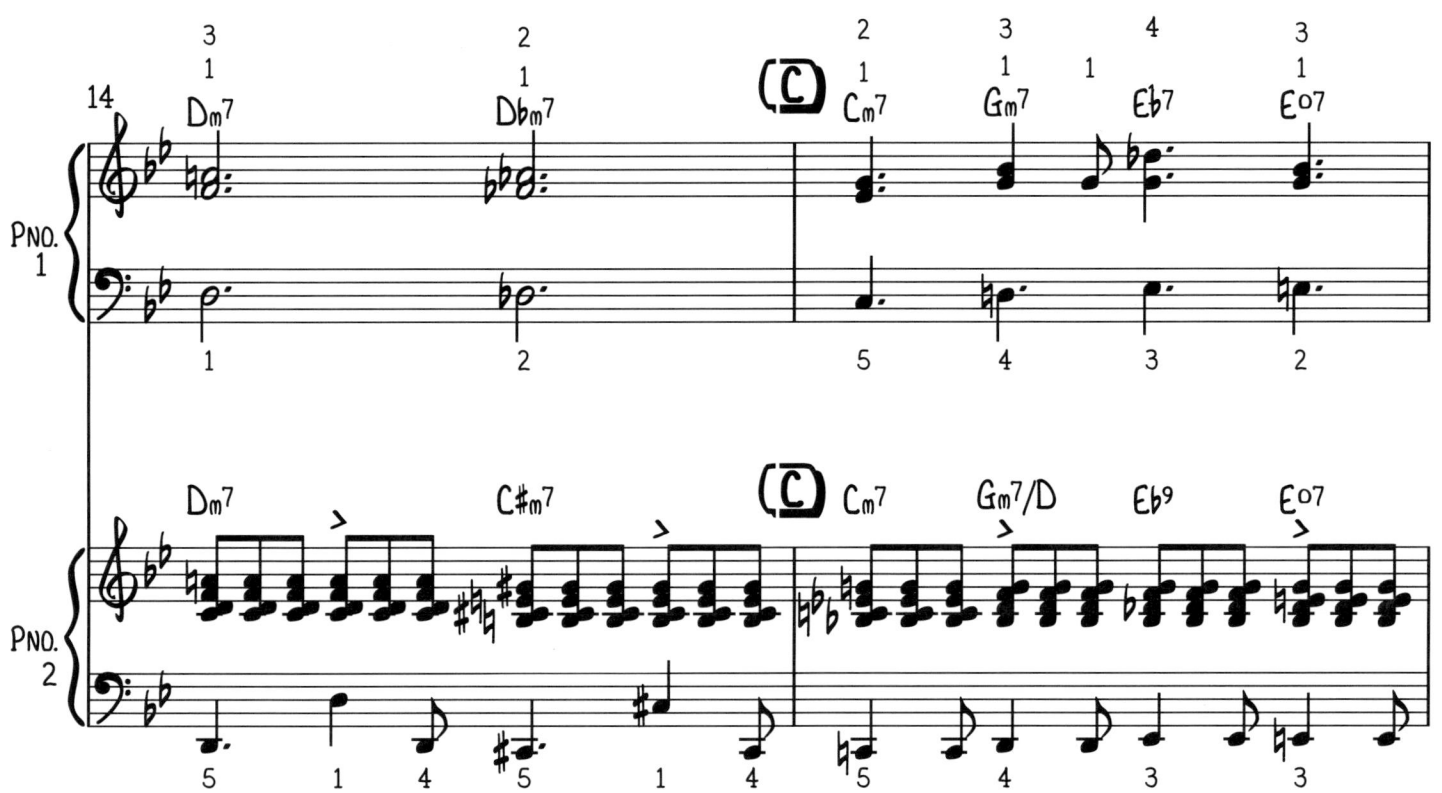

Note that the faster the tempo, the straighter the eighth notes, and the slower the tempo, the more unevenly played or exaggerated are the eighth notes. Most of the blues songs in this book are to be played using "swing eighth" notes, unless otherwise specified to use "straight eighths." The straight-eighth rhythmic feel is used in many contemporary blues and rock bands.

## VIII. IMPROVISING THE BLUES

As stated earlier, most blues melodies are based on the notes of the blues scale. (See Example 2). You can create or improvise melodies over the basic blues chord progression using short motives of one measure in length. You can begin by outlining the notes in the chord for playing melodies, as cited in the next example.

**Example 40: Improvising: Outlining Chords**

# IMPROVISING: OUTLINING CHORDS

Another way to improvise melodies is to use notes typically found in the blues: the flatted third, flatted fifth, and flatted seventh.

**Example 41: Improvising: Using the Blues Scale**

# IMPROVISING: USING THE BLUES SCALE

Improvise a blues melody using notes from the B♭ blues scale.

# B-FLAT BLUES SCALE

Improvise a blues melody using notes from the Bf blues scale. Add passing tones (notes that fall between chord tones), rolled chords, trills and short riffs. The riffs may be one, two or four measures in length. Remember that your solo must be expressive and have form and design.

**Example 42: Improvising: Rhythmic Approach**

When playing *I Can Do It Blues,* you should attempt to answer the other instruments in every other measure. When improvising, you can use notes of the blues scale, adding grace notes (blue notes), passing tones, rolled chords, trills, and short riffs.

**Example 43: I Can Do It Blues**

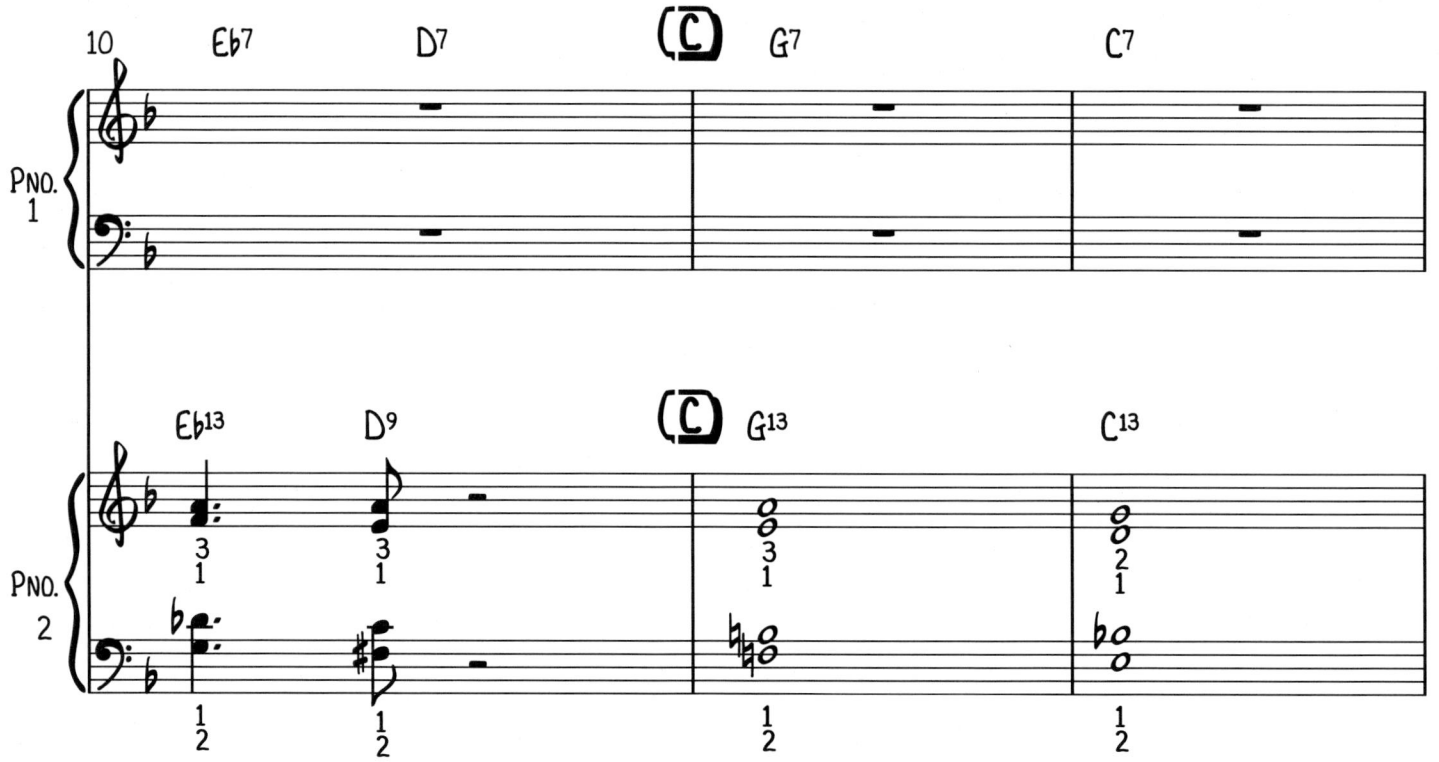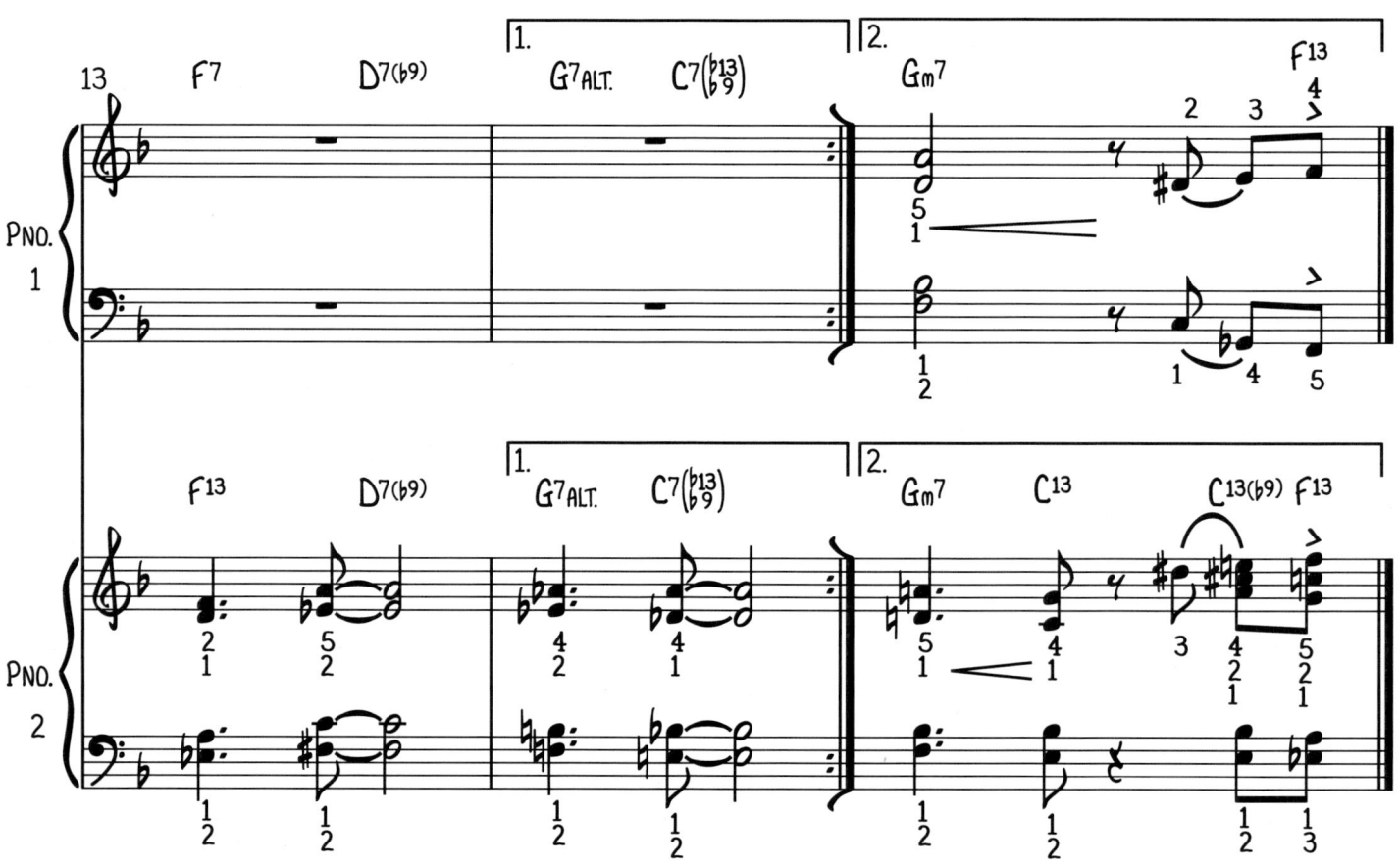

# IX. NEW CHORD PROGRESSIONS

To create variety in the chord structure you can use *filler* or *substitute* chords (a.k.a. substitutions) in the following ways:

## A. Example 44: Added Chords

The IV (subdominant) chord may be used in the second measure of a blues progression. The raised IV diminished seventh chord may be used on the second half of the second measure, and in measure six. The minor seventh chord functions as a subdominant or lead to the dominant seventh chord. It adds a new color and adds movement to the original chord. These added chords create a smoother bass line and easily connect the chords. Notice how certain bass notes are omitted from the right-hand voicing, providing a lighter sound. Observe how all dominant seventh chords contain the ninth for added tension.

# ADDED CHORDS

### B. Added Filler Chords

The IV7 chord or the IV 6/4 chord may be used as "filler" chords between two similar chords. These chords are referred to as "lifts" and provide variety and movement to the sound. Due to the quickness of the filler chords, the chords do not have to be supported by a different bass note. This type of filler sound is used a lot in gospel music.

**Example 45: Added Filler Chords**

1. A "walk-up" pattern can occur between two chords of the same name and between the I and the V7 chords. Notice that one note remains constant, while the other two notes move in parallel tenth intervals.

**Example 46: Walk-Up Connecting Pattern**

# WALK-UP CONNECTING PATTERN

A "walk-down" pattern can also be used for variety when the I chord moves to the V7 chord.

**Example 48: Walk-Down Connecting Pattern**

# WALK-DOWN CONNECTING PATTERN

The next song uses trills, grace notes, substitute chords, chromatic lines, and a more active chord progression.

**Example 49: Bouncing Baby Blues**

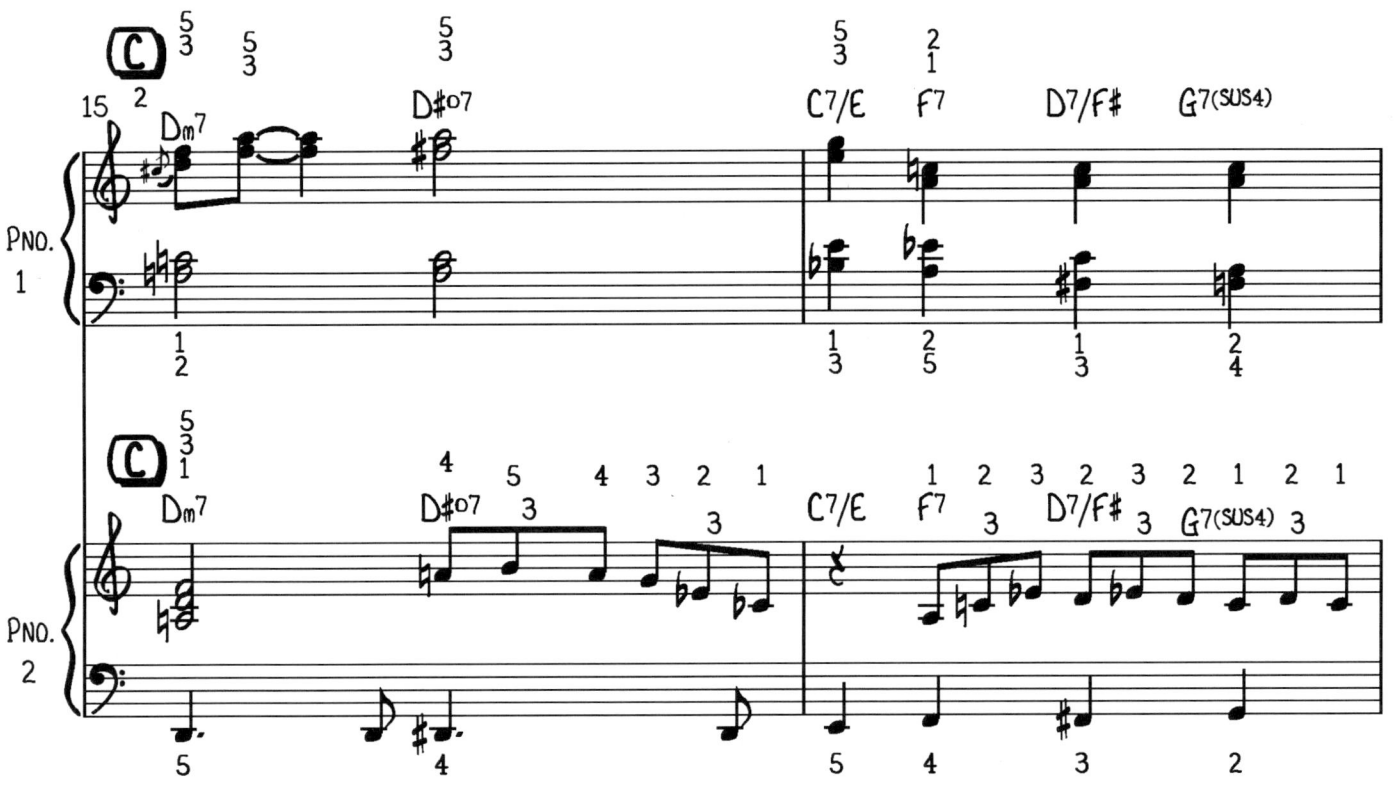

## X. BLUES IN A MINOR KEY

Blues can also be written in a minor key. Every major key has a *relative minor* key. For example, F major and D minor (same key signature), C major and A minor; B♭ major and G minor, and G major and E minor. You can locate the relative minor by selecting the sixth degree of the major scale and build a scale from that tone upwards. The most commonly used chords in minor are the minor I chord, the minor IV chord, and the dominant V7 chord.

# MINOR BLUES SCALE - D MINOR

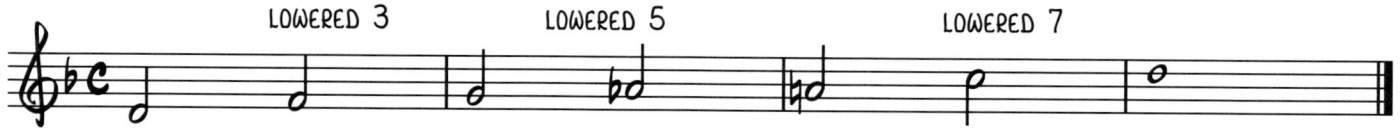

The next song uses the notes of the minor blues scale, grace notes, and blue notes. It should be performed in a 12/8 swing style.

**Example 50: Funky Frog Blues**

# FUNKY FROG BLUES

♩ = 126
KEY OF D MINOR
FUNKY GROOVE

BY VINCE COROZINE

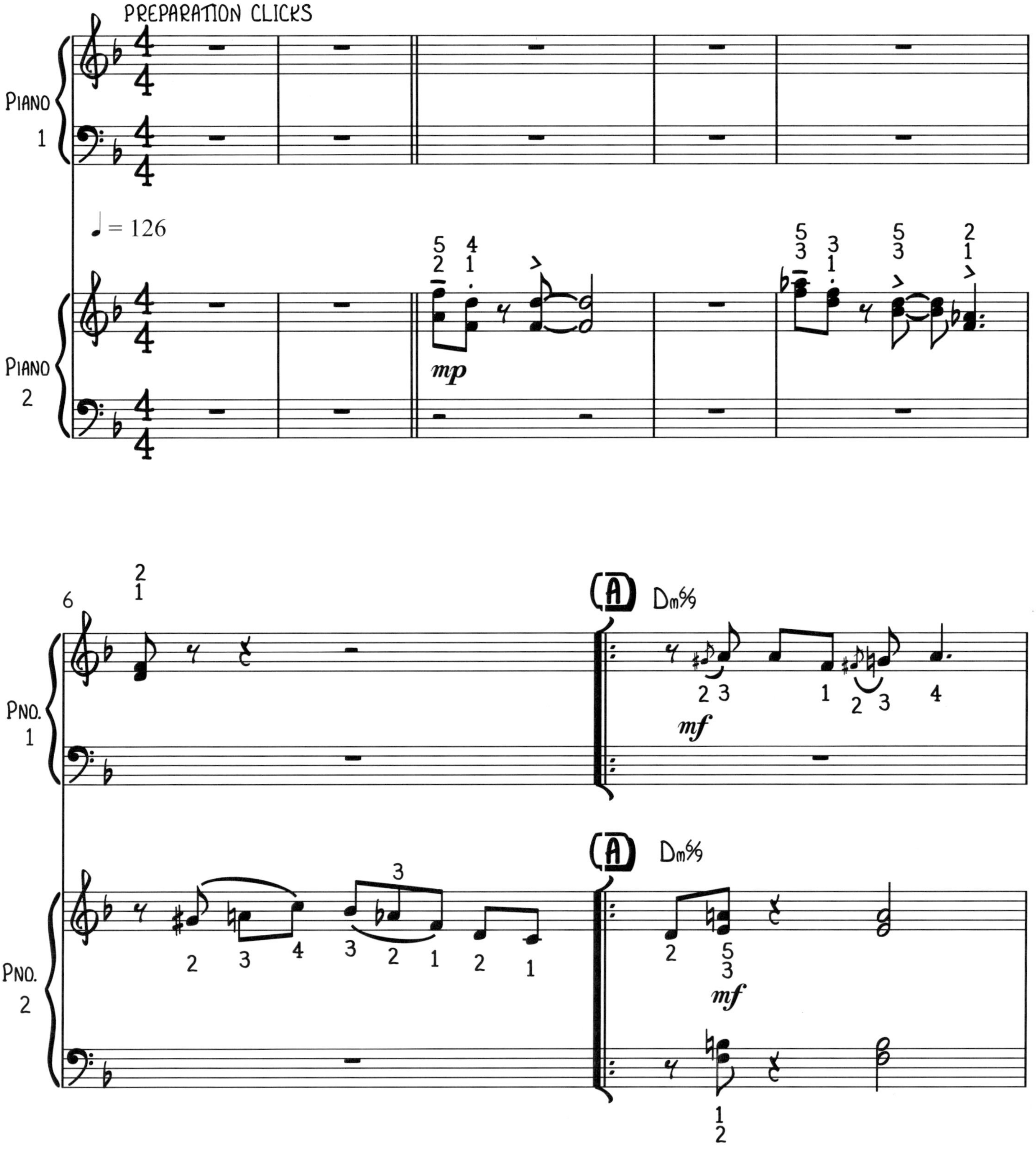

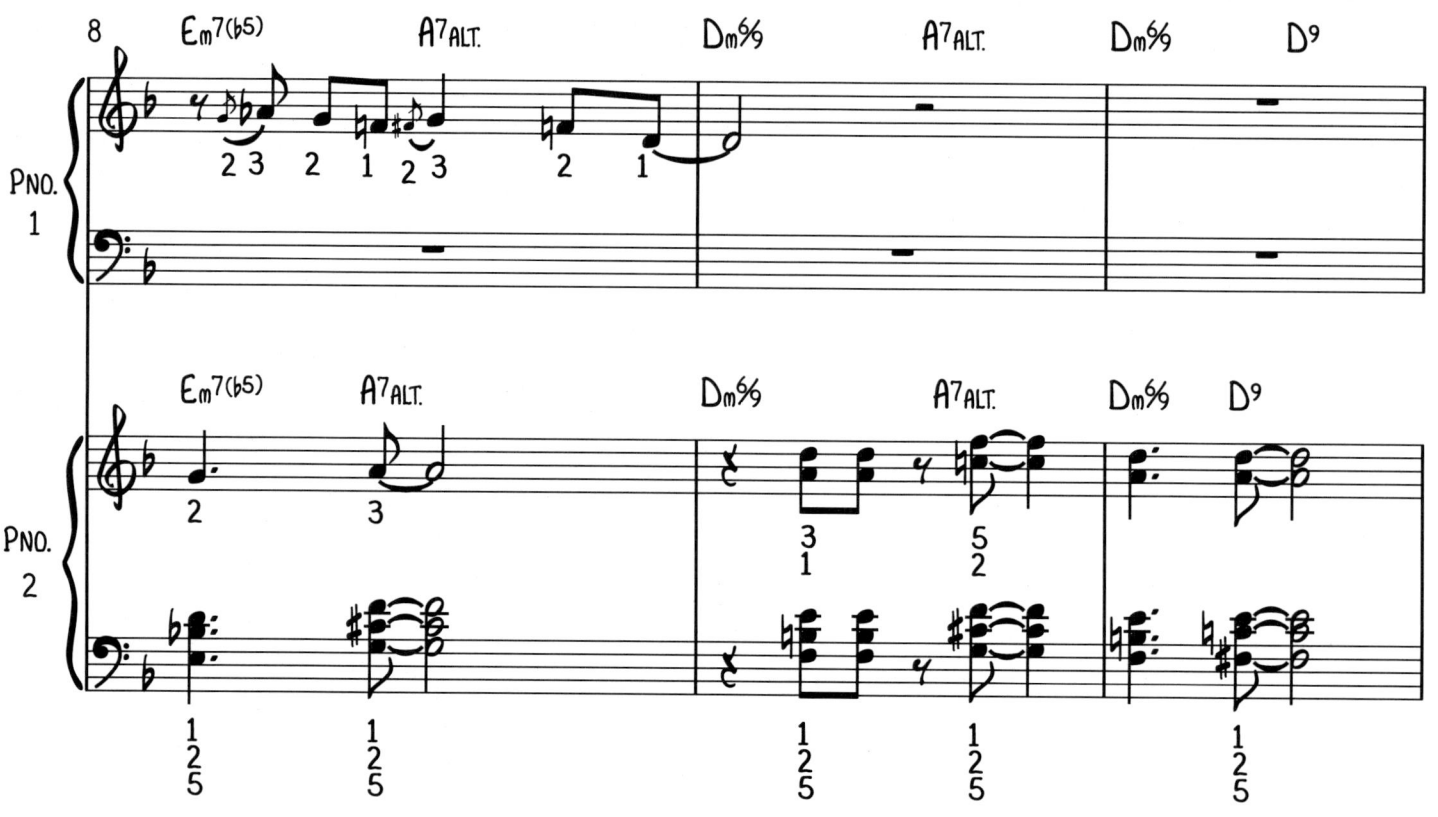

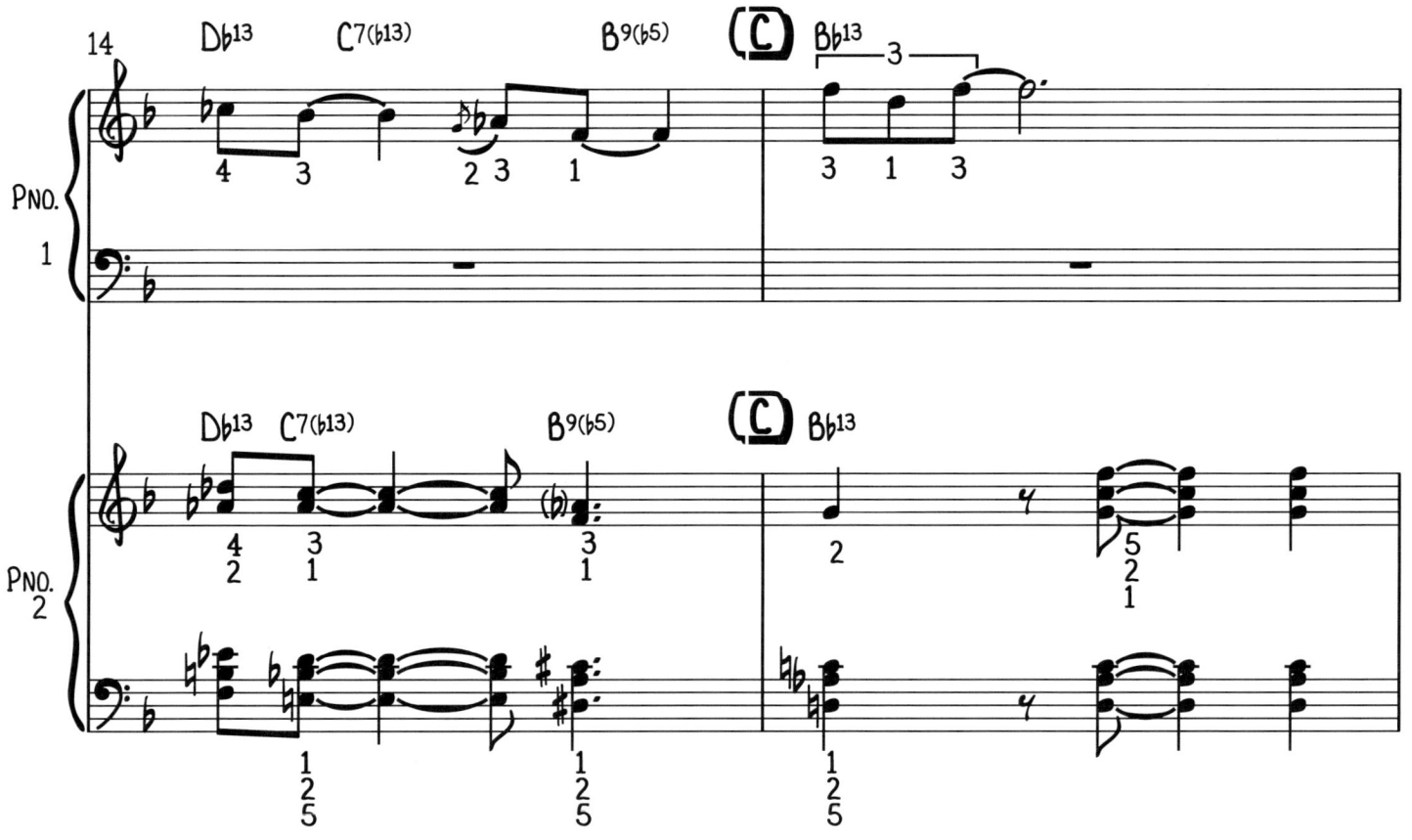

# APPENDIX A: Blues and Country Fills

# BLUES AND COUNTRY FILLS

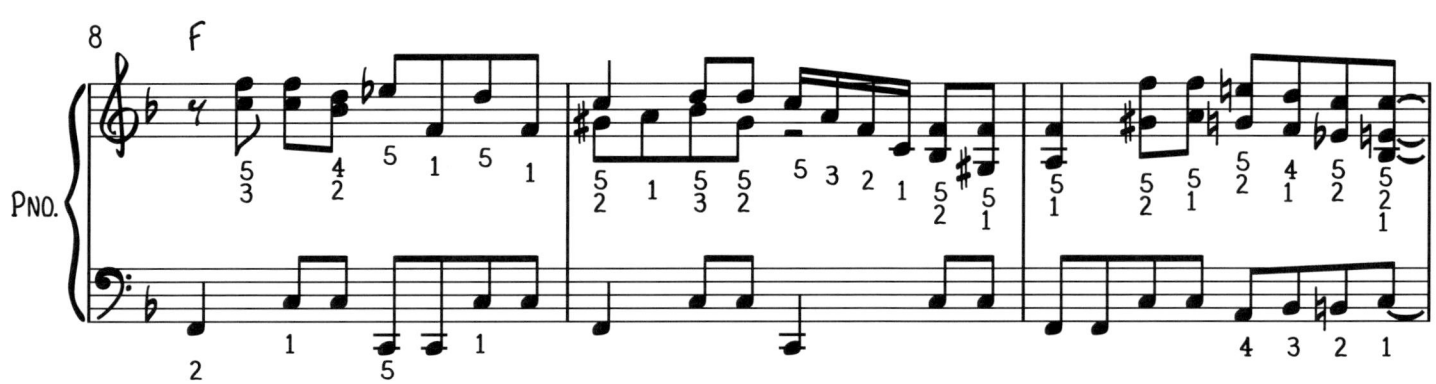
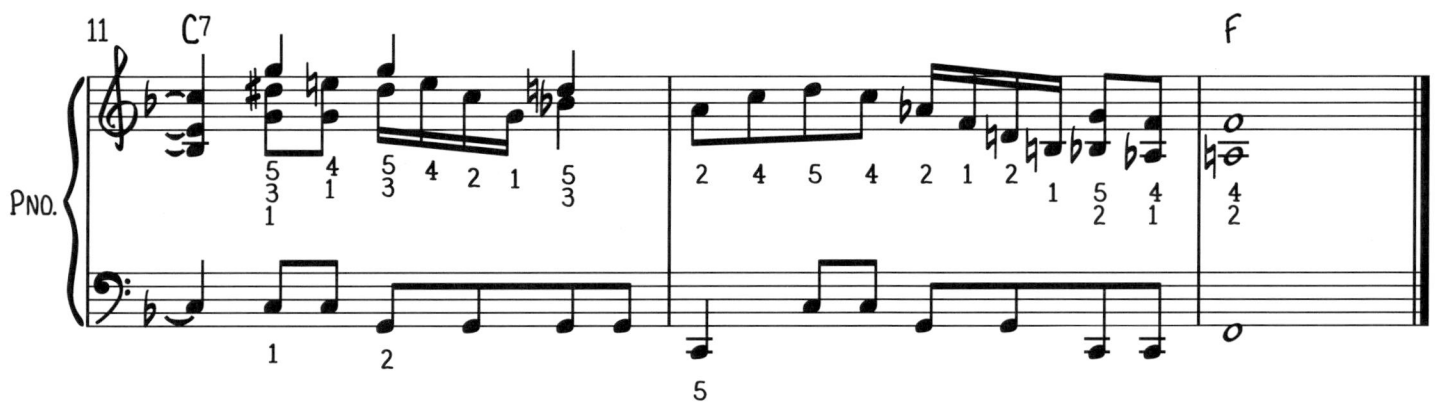

# APPENDIX B: Four Blues Choruses

This example is for listening and analysis. There are four, 12-bar blues choruses in the next example, beginning at letters A, B, C and D.

# FOUR BLUES CHORUSES

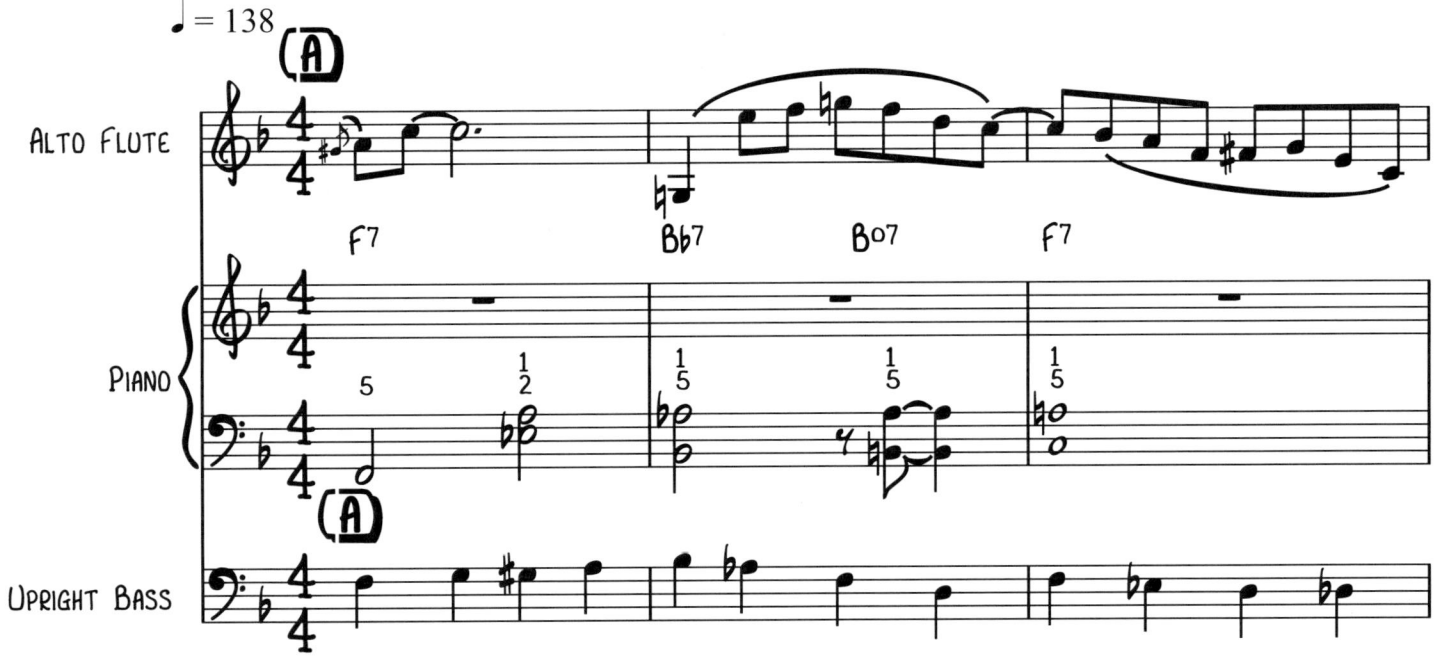

95

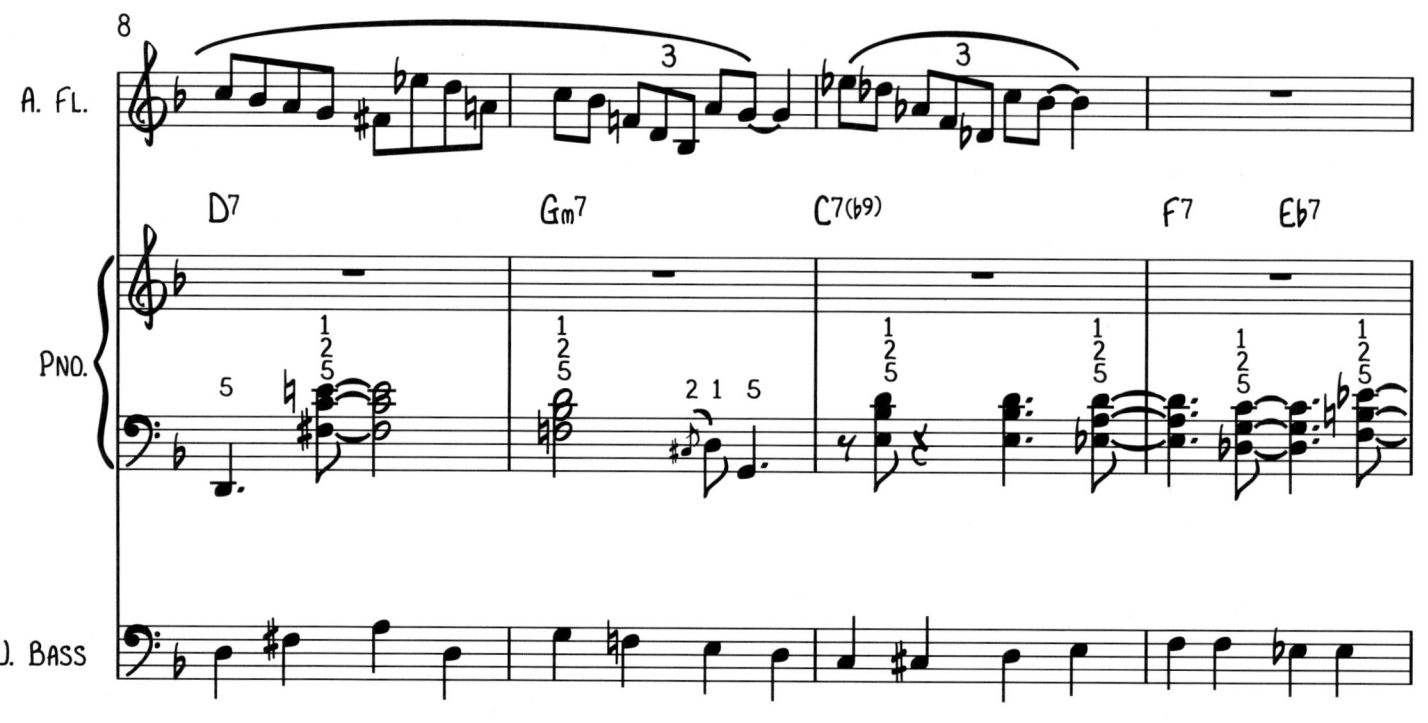

97

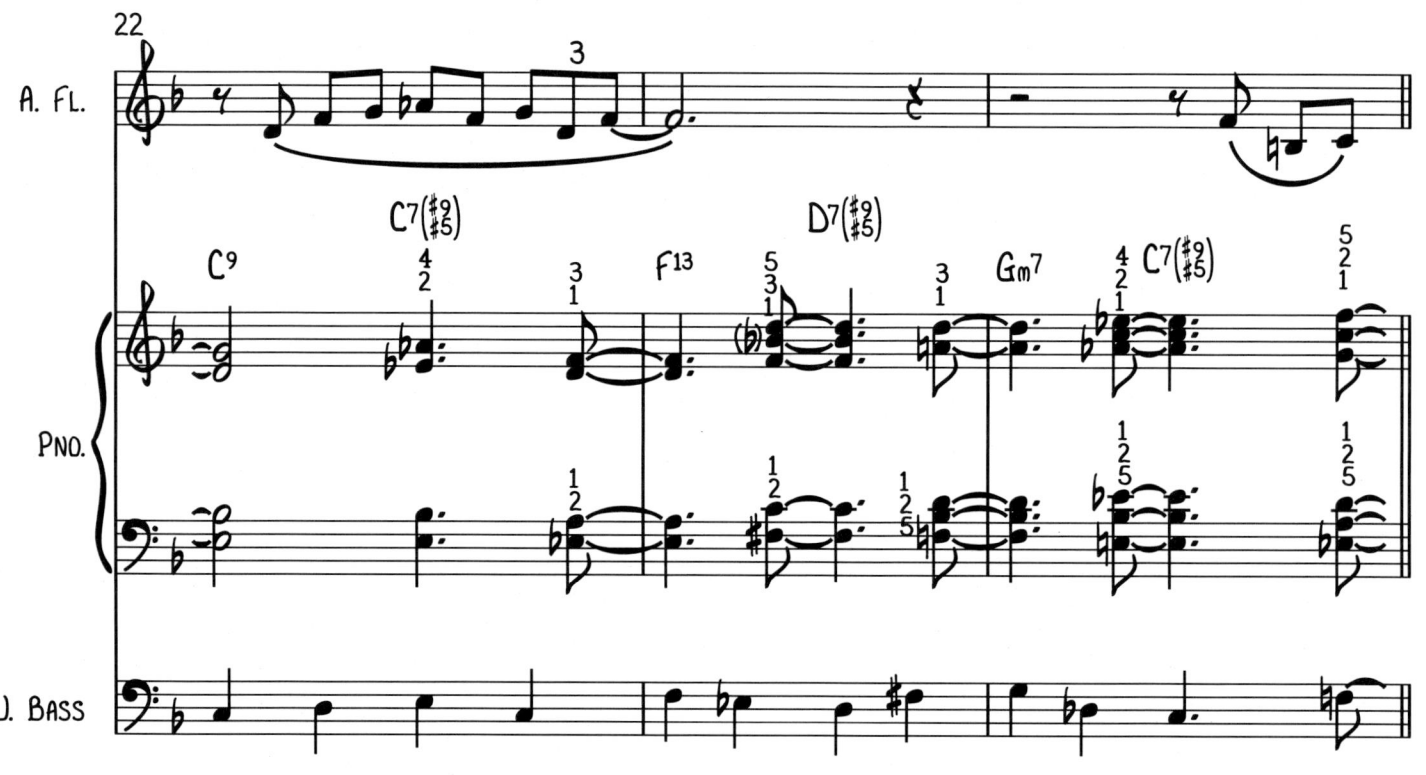

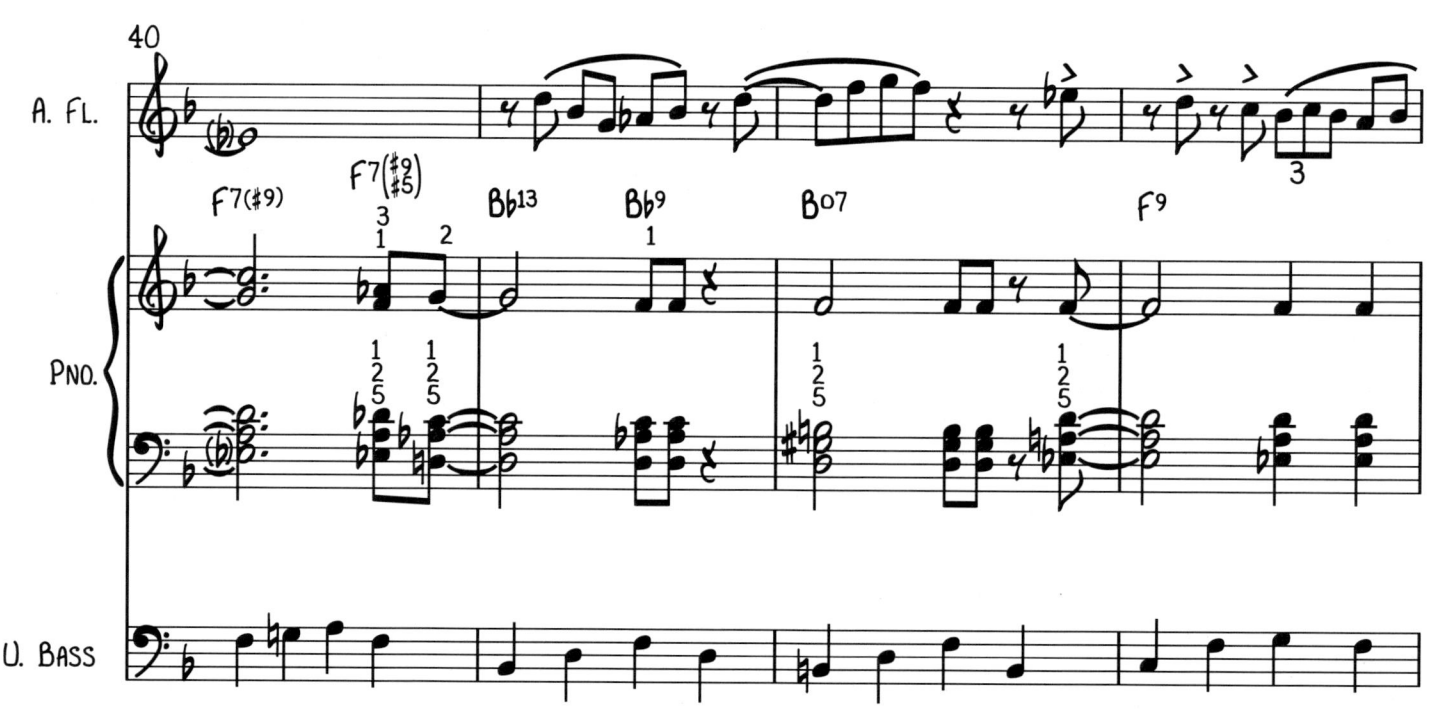

# APPENDIX C: Comping

"Comping" is a jazz term that refers to accompaniment for an instrumental soloist or vocalist. The pianist's task is to provide harmonic basis for the song, and keep it rhythmically interesting. Chord voicings tend to grow in size as the solo builds in intensity.

## Comping Tastefully Behind a Soloist

In order to "comp" tastefully behind a soloist, you must:

- Know the structure (chord changes) of the song.
- Know the form; AABA, blues, and so on.
- Be able to quickly select substitute chords and high-tension notes.
- Select diverse voicings for chords to avoid monotony. To "voice" refers to the way a keyboardist constructs his or her chords.
- Listen to what everybody (bass, drums, and soloist) is doing.

Your job is to make the soloist feel comfortable and sound better, and to create a feeling of dialogue with the soloist.

## Voicing Chords

Most keyboardists voice their chords to ensure that the top note of the right hand chord does not clash with the melody note of the song. Play the melody only if the soloist get lost, or if the vocalist has difficulty singing in tune.

When the melody contains a lot of movement or when the player plays "outside" of the chord changes of the tune (like trumpeter Woody Shaw), it is best to use fewer notes in the chords, **playing sparsely** and eliminating the root of the chord. Voicing chords in fourths and using chromatic fill-in chords usually works best in this type of situation.

For added tonal color, approach each chord by half step from above or below. Parallel diatonic or chromatic movement (passing chords) is effective when approaching chords.

## Hints for Effective "Comping"

1. Use repetition; too much variety becomes confusing.
2. When in doubt, don't play (lay out).
3. Strive to listen and anticipate what the soloist might do.
4. Play beneath the volume of the soloist.
5. Don't arpeggiate or roll chords.
6. Most "comping" should consist of **short, punctuated rhythms** that fill-in empty holes or compliment sustained notes played by the soloist. The use of offbeat rhythmic accents is desirable.

## Playing with a Bass

Remember to comp very sparingly behind a bass soloist. Use light, sparse voicings in a higher register. You don't have to play the roots of the chords if a bass player is present. When playing a ballad, the keyboardist gets a chance to explore chromatic linear motion inside the voicings. The comping behind a bassist usually contains long, sustained sounds.

## Transitions from Latin to Jazz

Transitions from one feel to another (Latin to Jazz or vice versa) are made smoothly, usually starting a bar or two before the next section actually begins. The final "out chorus" is an ideal place for the keyboardist to comp in a much more active way by using powerful chord voicings.

# APPENDIX D: Practice Tips

Practicing an instrunent is the most important thing you can do to improve your musical skills. The French word for "practice" or "rehearsal" is "repetition," and repetition develops muscle memory. The learning process is a continuous journey of discovery.

## Warm-Up

Similar to any sport, playing a musical instrument requires muscle warm-ups. Instead of stretching leg, back and arm muscles for a workout, you will need to practice and focus on your hand muscles to develop kinetic memory. To build muscle memory in your hands, you need to warm up by playing scales and arpeggios. This repetition will build muscle memory gain. Rhythmic repetition and finger dexterity are essential for playing jazz. Build those muscles!

## Place

Practice in a place that has proper lighting and ventilation with no distractions.

## Time

Make practice time a daily routine of at least thirty minutes per day. The thirty minutes may be broken into two, fifteen-minute sessions to avoid fatigue. Practicing at the same time each day will ensure the habit of regular practice and advancement. Practice also occurs as the pianist listens to recordings, reads books and scores, and interacts with other musicians.

## Goals

Set an obtainable goal for each rehearsal period. Set a target goal that you know you can attain. Such items as smooth connections of musical lines, accurate technique, playing chords without hesitation, playing scales evenly, phrasing, playing in time with the audio, memorizing patterns that accompany chords, learning one song per week, and so on, are achievable goals to set. Listening to the recordings of professional pianists is also essential to one's learning process. A jazz pianist should not end a practice session without achieving his/her goals for that particular session.

## How to Practice

It is best to **practice slowly and accurately**, particularly with the trouble spots you are having. This approach will allow your hand muscles and fingers to learn the patterns practiced. It is best to play the pattern or exercise at least ten times consecutively with no errors. This will help you to play with less effort and tension and promote consistency in your playing. Most students find that playing scales and arpeggios **using a metronome** helps them to execute the notes in proper time. Remember, the goals of practice are to build accuracy, confidence, and muscle memory, and to have fun!

# APPENDIX E: Chord Symbols Used in this Book

Maj7   Major triad with a major seventh added

m7     Minor triad with a minor seventh added

6       Major or minor triad with a major sixth added

♯5     Chord with a raised fifth (same as augmented fifth)

7       Major triad with a minor seventh added

o7     Diminished seventh (series of minor 3rds)

9       Chord with major ninth added (same as second)

♭9     Chord with a lowered 9th

♯9     Chord with a raised 9th (same as flatted $10^{th}$)

13     Dominant seventh chord with added thirteenth (same as sixth)

susp   Chord with a suspended fourth (raised $3^{rd}$)

m7♭5  Minor seventh chord with a lowered fifth

♯11    Chord with a raised eleventh ($4^{th}$)

B♭/F   B-flat triad with F in the bass

G/D   G triad with D in the bass

# APPENDIX F: What Makes a Good Jazz Solo?

Improvisation not only applies to the creation of melodic lines, but also to the spontaneous expression of chord voicings, re-harmonization, rhythmic ideas, form, and other elements of music.

When playing jazz, the number of notes you play is not as important as how and where you play them. This is called *taste*. Taste requires hours of practice and careful listening to develop. Taste also involves selecting the proper placement of notes. It is a balance of overstatement and understatement.

Fast technique is acceptable if it says something musical. Playing high, loud, and fast has its moments, but you should use them as an exception rather than the rule.

- Judge the mood of the piece and add your own personal feeling to the music. Begin with a simple idea or motive, and develop it as you play.

- Repeat an idea more than once, (this adds continuity) and don't wander aimlessly from one idea to another.

- Use "open" spaces (no playing) to set up your next idea. This provides interest. Let the rhythm section work between ideas.

- Build tension and excitement. Start simply and build to a climax. When you run out of ideas and have nothing more to say-**STOP**!

- Develop rhythmic variety and a mixture of dynamics (first chorus *p* and the second chorus *f*) and use crescendos and diminuendos for added interest.

- Try playing scales creatively; up or down, or begin in the middle and go either way.

- Listen to the rhythm section and "ride" the time. Keep the constant feeling of the hi-hat cymbals and bass part in your head at all times. Playing the "time" is more important than the notes you play. If you can't think of anything to play—wait and listen to the rhythm section—let them spur you on. Lean on them; talk to them...

- Aim for a relaxed, *legato* flow to your sound. Imply a feeling of forward motion in everything you do. Sound like you mean it! Tension clouds your thinking, so think free! Be mindful that phrasing IS important.

- Remember that sustained notes give a player a chance to think of what to play next, and give the listener a chance to absorb what he/she has just heard. Nothing is as dull as a jazz solo that fills up every beat with notes and more notes. Fight the urge to fill it up.

- Incorporate material from the song and save your best "shot" for the end.

# APPENDIX G: Jazz Pianists Every Student Should Hear

Kenny Barron
Jaki Byard
Michael Cochrane
Chick Corea
Kenny Drew
Bill Evans
Clare Fischer
Tommy Flanagan
Red Garland
Benny Green
Al Haig
Herbie Hancock
Hampton Hawes
Keith Jarrett
Hank Jones
Wynton Kelly
Kenny Kirkland

Diana Krall
John Lewis
Brad Mehldau
Mulgrew Miller
Johnny Morris
Phineas Newborn, Jr.
Oscar Peterson
Bud Powell
Horace Silver
Art Tatum
Bobby Timmons
Lennie Tristano
McCoy Tyner
Cedar Walton
Randy Weston
Mary Lou Williams
Teddy Wilson

# APPENDIX H: Glossary of Jazz Terms Used in this Book

**1. Anticipation:** A rhythmic device or alteration where accents fall on subdivisions of the bar not normally stressed.

**2. Blues:** A 12-bar pattern, in the AAB form, that employs the use of the I, IV and V chords. A call-and-response pattern employing the use of "blue notes."

**3. Blues Scale:** Alteration of the major scale through lowering the third, fifth and seventh a half-step.

**4. Blue Notes:** Notes that are altered or lowered in the scale, creating a momentary dissonance within the chord.

**5. Chord Inversions:** When a note other than the root of the chord appears in the bass or as the lowest voice without affecting the chord quality. Used to create smooth voice-leading and a more interesting bass line.

**6. Comping:** Accompaniment using rhythmic patterns and chords to back-up a singer or an instrumentalist.

**7. Contrary Motion:** Two voices moving in opposite directions.

**8. Drone Notes:** Notes that are continuously sounded or repeated while other notes move above or below.

**9. Filler Chords:** Chords that are played between the most prominent chords in a song.

**10. Grace Notes:** Short, slurred notes that are quickly played just prior to a note that is accented.

**11. Improvisation:** On-the-spot creation of a part that fits the given chord progression.

**12. Pedal-Point:** A sustained or repeated note, usually in the bass, while various chords are played over it.

**13. Pentatonic Scale:** A five-tone scale with no half-steps, containing the first, second, fourth, fifth and seventh note of the natural minor scale.

**14. Riff:** A short, syncopated repeated phrase that creates a feeling of forward motion and excitement behind a soloist.

**15. Shell "Guide-Tone" Voicings:** Playing only the root, third and seventh of a chord, or playing the root and third, or the third and the seventh. These notes are played with the pianist's left hand, creating an open-sounding chord.

**16. Slash Chords:** A compound chord that indicates that a chord is to be played over a certain bass note. A pitch other than the root is thus in the bass. For example, B♭/C means that one will play a B♭ triad over a C bass note.

**17. Straight Eighths:** Eighth notes that are played "straight" (evenly) and not with a "swing" feeling. This is typical for Latin, rock and classical music.

**18. Stride Piano:** A style of piano playing that requires the left hand to move very quickly between a single accented bass note and the chord that follows; the effect is an "oompah-like" rhythm.

**19. Syncopation:** Shifting an accent from a strong beat or part of a beat to a weak beat or part of a beat, where the accent wouldn't normally occur.

**20. Swing Eighths:** Eighth notes played with a 12/8, uneven feeling.

**21. Turnaround:** A two-measure phrase used for endings that go back to the main melody.

**22. Trill (Shake):** A rapid alteration between two adjacent notes, usually a whole-step or half-step apart.

**23. Voicing:** A specific allocation of chord tones between the hands, chosen to interpret the chord in question.

**24. Walk-Up Pattern:** Movement in the bass that walks up the scale to the next chord.

**25. Walk-Down Pattern:** Movement in the bass that walks down the scale to the next chord.

**26. Walking Bass Line:** A bass line played with quarter notes on all four beats of the measure.

# APPENDIX I: Blues Songs to Learn

Au Privave
Bag's Groove
Barbados
Bessie's Blues
Billie's Bounce
Bloomdido
Blue Monk
Blue Train
Blues for Alice
C Jam Blues
Chasin' the Trane
Cheryl Blues
Cool Blues
Doodlin'
Five Spot After Dark
Footprints
Freddie the Freeloader
Israel
K.C. Blues
Limehouse Blues
Now's the Time
Opus de Funk
Parker's Mood
Route 66
Sandu
Solar
Sonnymoon for Two
St. Louis Blues
Straight, No Chaser
Tenor Madness
Things Ain't What They Used to Be
Viered Blues
Walkin'
West Coast Blues

# APPENDIX J: Select Bibliography of Blues Books

Richards, Tim. *Improvising Blues Piano,* Schott Music, 1997.

Dennis, Matt. *Blues Piano Styles,* Mel Bay Publications, Inc., 1973.

Dennis, Matt. *Introduction to the Blues,* Mel Bay Publications, Inc., 1976.

Konowitz, Bert. *Nothing But the Blues,* Alfred Music, 2000.

# APPENDIX K: Select Bibliography of Jazz Improvisation Books

Abersole, Jamey. *Jazz Piano Play-A-Long Sets, Volumes. 1-133,* New Albany, IN. Jamey Abersole Jazz Inc, 2000-2010.

Crook, Hal. *How to Improvise: An Approach to Practicing Improvisation,* Rottenburg, Germany. Advance Music, 1991.

Dobbins, Bill. *The Contemporary Jazz Pianist, A Comprehensive Approach to Keyboard Improvisation-Volumes* 1-4, New York, NY. Charles Colin Music, 1978-1989.

Haerle, Dan. *Jazz Improvisation for Keyboard Players,* Van Nuys, CA. Alfred Music, 1978.

Levine, Mark. *The Jazz Theory Book,* Petaluma, CA. Sher Music, 1995.

Meehegan, John F. *Improvising Jazz Piano,* New York, NY. Amsco Publications, 1985.

Meehegan, John F. *Jazz Improvisation: Volumes 1-4,* New York, NY. Watson-Guptill, 1959, 1962, 1964, and 1965.

Reeves, Scott D. *The Art of Piano Playing,* Wolfeboro, NH. Longwood Academic, 1973.

*Vince Corozine*

Vince Corozine grew up in New York and was Associate Professor of Music for 25 years at two universities in New York and in North Carolina.

He studied musical composition with Bernard Wagenaar of the Juilliard School of Music, with jazz composer Jimmy Giuffre, and film scoring with Don Sebesky.

Vince was the music arranger for the Jazz Knights at West Point for ten years, music director for the annual Thanksgiving Parade in Philadelphia, also for ten years, and has conducted members of the Toronto Symphony, Hong Kong Philharmonic Orchestra and Philly Pops in recording sessions.

He is the author of *Arranging Music for the Real World,* published by Mel Bay Publications, Inc. Presently, he teaches a dozen music composition and arranging courses online including: Music Theory I, II, III; Jazz Theory, Songwriting, Music Composition, Orchestration, Counterpoint, Jazz Arranging I (small groups) and Jazz Arranging II (large ensembles), and Choral Arranging.

As music director of the Norm Hathaway Big Band in New York, he has made appearances at the Iridium Jazz Club on Broadway in New York City and a special appearance on *Saturday Night Live*.

Vince was inducted into the Blues Hall of Fame in 2013.

**WWW.MELBAY.COM**